HOW TO
PRAY
FOR SOMEONE
YOU LOVE

HOW TO
PRAY
FOR SOMEONE
YOU LOVE

BRUCE DOWNES

WINTERS
PUBLISHING GROUP

Published by Winters Publishing, LLC
2448 E. 81st St. Suite #4802 | Tulsa, Oklahoma 74137 USA

Book design copyright © 2017 by Winters Publishing, LLC. All rights reserved.
Layout Design by Christina Hicks Creative
www.christinahickscreative.com

Published in the United States of America

ISBN: 978-1-947-42-6801

DEDICATION

To those who ask God
to act in the lives of those they Love.

God has already read your heart.

Your prayers, your truest desires have
already been heard in heaven.

God is on the way.

No!

God is here!

Table of Contents

ACKNOWLEDGEMENTS 9

HOW TO PRAY FOR SOMEONE

YOU LOVE 11

PART 1: A FEW THOUGHTS ON PRAYER 17

PART 2: WHO AM I PRAYING FOR 31

PART 3: SCRIPTURE TO HELP US PRAY 35

PART 4: A DAILY QUOTE FROM

THE SAINTS 41

PART 5: PRAYERS OLD AND NEW 51
   THE CATHOLIC GUY RULE OF LIFE
   DAILY PRAYER. 51
   PRAYERS FOR INTENTIONS
   AND NEEDS 53
   BIBLICAL PRAYERS 93
   FAMILY PRAYERS 97
   PRAYERS FOR HEALING 116
   HOLY SPIRIT PRAYERS 141
   PRAYERS FOR PEACE 156
CATHOLIC PRAYERS 158
   PRAYERS FOR THE CHURCH 174
   PRAYERS FOR MARY'S
   INTERCESSION 178
   PRAYERS OF THE SAINTS 186
   MASS PRAYERS 198

PRAYERS BEFORE HOLY
COMMUNION 198
PRAYERS AFTER HOLY
COMMUNION 199
CONFESSION/RECONCILIATION
PRAYERS 203
MORNING PRAYERS 208
ADVENT PRAYERS 210
CHRISTMAS PRAYERS. 214
PRAYERS FOR EASTER 219
"ACTS OF" PRAYERS 221

ACKNOWLEDGEMENTS

Thank you Sandra Purcell and Rosemary Downes for your help again.

You both do so much to make this ministry effective in proclaiming Jesus to our world.

ACKNOWLEDGMENTS

HOW TO PRAY FOR SOMEONE YOU LOVE

Will you pray for my mum?

Will you pray for my friend?

Will you pray for my child?

Will you pray for my wife?

Will you pray for my husband?

Will you pray for a colleague at work?

Will you pray for me?

Every day they pour in from around the world. Prayers requests. Every time I go somewhere to speak, people approach me and ask me to pray.

It is as if my prayers are somehow extra special, that I am connected to God in a way that others are not. But this is not true, my prayers are just like yours. I cannot change anything, but I know that God can.

I have had the great privilege to see God answer prayers over and over, and this has brought me to believe that he can answer your prayers with a precision and wisdom beyond anything we have.

Right now, God knows why you are reading this book called *How to Pray for Someone You Love*.

God already knows who you are praying for and who you are going to pray for as we start this journey.

By picking up this book and watching the videos that go with it, you are stepping onto the waters of faith and trusting that God will meet the needs of those you are praying for.

Do not be surprised if you are also changed by this journey, however.

Before we begin, I should I also say that God wants you to love yourself. The Scriptures (Bible) tells us that we are called to look after ourselves in body, mind and spirit. It is an obligation that we all have.

You may actually be the Someone You Love that you are praying for.

HOW WE ARE GOING TO PRAY FOR SOMEONE YOU LOVE

This book is written to be done over a 31 day period as we Pray for Someone We Love. It will be a dedicated time when we can be aware from the time we wake until we sleep and for the whole 31 days that we are holding up to God for His blessing and grace the people listed in Part 2 - WHO I AM PRAYING FOR.

DAILY VIDEO

In conjunction with this, you can view a 5-minute video each day for 31 days that will help you to pray.

The videos will be sent by email one day at a time from the time you start.

DAILY PRAY FOR SOMEONE YOU LOVE VIDEOS
You may want to read Parts 1 to 3 of this book before you register, as the videos will start the day after you register. To receive the videos, register here;

https://TheCatholicGuy.com/PrayforSomeone

HOW TO READ THIS BOOK

This book comprises five parts:

Part 1: A few thoughts on prayer to help us pray.

I strongly recommend that you read Part 1 before you begin. It aims to prepare your heart for *How to Pray For Someone You Love*.

Part 2: Who I am praying for.

Write in this section those you are praying for and what you are praying for if you have a specific intention in mind for them. Be careful what you write as others may read this.

Part 3: Scripture to help us pray.

The Scripture is God's word to us or as the Catechism of the Catholic Church says of the Scripture, it is God coming to talk to us. Each day there is a passage that you can read and reflect upon. I will help you to do this should you not be sure how.

Part 4: A daily quote from a saint.

The saints were women and men who lived lives of dedication to God. By their lives they point to God, and we can learn how we to can respond to God from their actions and words.

Part 5: Prayers old and new.

Sometimes we may not know what to say to God. There are prayers some centuries old that when read (prayed) capture exactly what we would like to say. They are an aid to our heart's prayer.

I strongly recommend that you read Part 1 before you begin.

PART 1: A FEW THOUGHTS ON PRAYER

WHAT IS PRAYER?

Now this is a great question.

When we boil it down, prayer at its basic essence is talking to God, listening to God and being in each other's presence.

Saint Thérèse of Lisieux said of prayer:

For me, prayer is a surge of the heart; it is a simple look turned toward heaven, it is a cry of recognition and of love, embracing both trial and joy.
Prayer is about a relationship that is not one where we do the asking and God does the giving, but rather is an interplay between us as human beings and God who created us, who also wants to relate to us, guide us, love

us and ultimately lead us to Him. It is about a personal, individual, intimate relationship that has a uniqueness to it because each of us is uniquely made by God.

This relationship is also not just about knowing things about God and being able to describe what God has done, but rather is about knowing God personally as our friend, Saviour and Lord.

Many of us can describe the things we believe God has done, but that is different to being able to describe God as someone we know for ourselves.

This relationship is not just about you and God alone, but rather is part of a family called the Church, the people of God, who have a history and a story, who are our spiritual family, even if we don't feel we know them at times.

God, who is Father and Mother, is close. Very close. It says in Genesis that we are made in His image and likeness. Male and female, he created us.

When we talk about God and to God, we so often speak in the masculine. I know I do all the time, but God is equally feminine with all of the qualities of life-giving, nurture and strength that we associate with femininity.

Prayer is not about the future alone but is also about now, and the 'yesterday' you carry within you now and into the future. It is about here, right now where you at this very moment.

There is nothing that we can say to God that He does not know. He sees everything. He has always been a part of your life whether you acknowledge Him or been aware of Him.

God exists regardless of whether you believe or not.

Knowing how to pray is not unique to you or me. One day a disciple, a follower of Jesus, came and asked him in Luke 11:1:

He was praying in a certain place, and after he had finished, one of his disciples said to him, "Lord, teach us to pray, as John taught his disciples."
The Scripture and tradition of the Church teach us that prayer needs to be learnt. It is not that we cannot just talk outright to God,

of course we can, but deepening a relationship takes effort, wisdom and experience for it to become fully effective in us.

The easiest kind of prayer is what I call the "list prayer," or the "give me prayer." This is where we come to God with our list and tell God all we want to happen for us, those we love and circumstances in our world. There is nothing wrong with this kind of asking prayer because it acknowledges the greatness of God and that He alone can provide these things.

In itself, if we realize what we are doing, that is putting our needs before God and is, therefore, one of the highest forms of worship as it recognizes God's amazing nature to be above all and affect all things.

Just asking God for 'stuff' and to do 'stuff,' however, is not a balanced relationship.

We can think that prayer comes from our mind. That it is a decision of the will and while that is true, prayer comes from a much deeper place, and that place is our heart. The Scripture talks of the heart over 1,000 times when it comes to prayer. Prayer is from the whole of us, or we might say the center of us, or we might say from that place where we are, our truest self – the heart.

The core of us, which is that place that people often do not see, we might also describe as our heart. Our head and hands can mean well, but they can be frail. For example, I love my wife Rosemary more than anyone, but I can be terrible to her at times. My heart means well, but my thoughts and actions, my head and my hands, can do something else than what is in my heart.

Prayer comes from that center point within us that is our truest self. It is the reason your prayers, which come from the center of you, are so meaningful. They are sincere.

For us to grow in our relationship with God, prayer from our heart needs to become a deliberate habit. It cannot be accidental or even from time to time.

Years ago, I was taught by my mentor in prayer, Fr Des Williamson, the need to pray consistently. He would tell me to pray for 15 minutes a day, not in the shower or lying down, or in front of the television, but to make a deliberate decision to set up my life so that I could spend 15 minutes of uninterrupted time with God. Fifteen minutes does not seem much, but 15 minutes when you live a busy life can be a challenge to find every day.

Depending on what season I was at in life, this sometimes meant it was done early in the morning before I started the day or at night. All he would say was do it when you are at your best and are capable of being fully present to God. I describe this in greater detail in my book Personal Prayer.

Many of us pray when we need something, but when times are good, prayer can be absent from our lives. This is not the way any healthy relationship works, but God understands that in many ways we are still growing.

Any of us who have had children know what it is like to see our children become independent. As they set up their own life, they spend less and less time with us as they learn to provide for themselves and pursue their life's goals. Many of us also know that call on the telephone or unexpected visit accompanied by the words, "Mum, dad can I borrow…"

As parents, we might be able to help, or we might not because of our limitations, but that does not mean we reject our children. God never rejects us even if we do not receive what we ask.

An authentic decision to pray is very much one of the heart.

Through the Gospels, Jesus taught us that a conversion needs to take place in our heart before and as we pray so that we can be all that God is calling us to be and to experience Him ourselves. This conversion of heart that Jesus seeks concerns:

- Being reconciled to our brother and sister before we prayed

- Loving our enemies

- Praying for people who persecute us

- Praying in secret where no one else knows

- Asking sincere forgiveness of God for our failings

- Having a pure heart that is desiring God's will

Most of all, however, this conversion of heart has to do with seeking the Kingdom of God in our everyday lives above all else.

This conversion of heart, as outlined in what is known as the Sermon on the Mount, is about seeking after the Father's love and will for us. The list above is often counter-intuitive to that which we may want to do ourselves or even comes naturally to us.

It does not seem natural to forgive an enemy or pray for someone making like difficult for us, but to the person who has had a heart conversion as they surrender themselves to the will of God, it is power and peace.

It is in the conversion of our hearts that we begin to see differently. It is here where faith, which is that gift of trusting beyond what we see, takes over in ways that could not have come about in any other way but through prayer.

Now faith is the assurance of things hoped for, the conviction of things not seen.

Hebrews 11:1

PRAYER OF INTERCESSION

You are holding a book that is about praying for others, so why have I started by talking about you being a person of prayer and experiencing a conversion of heart? Let me answer this question with a story.

A few years ago, I was sitting at my desk when my phone rang. It was my oldest daughter Emma, who had dropped in my parents' home to visit. In a panic, she said, "Dad come. The ambulance is on its way. Pop (my Dad) came into the kitchen while I was talking with Gran and said he could not breathe. The ambulance is on its way. Come quickly."

I raced to the house just as they were putting him in the ambulance. Our eyes met, but he was not up to saying anything.

It turned out that years before when he had worked on merchant ships he had breathed in asbestos fiber that was wrapped around the hot pipes in the engine room. The asbestos fiber had been in his lungs but now had taken over and was hindering on an increasing basis his ability to breathe.

They put him on constant oxygen and initially were able to stabilize him to the point where, after some weeks, he was allowed to come home but remain on oxygen.

His prognosis was not good, however. They told us there was nothing that could be done. Dad was dying.

Just before he came home from hospital, my oldest brother Gary spoke to me and said that we had done the best we could medically but that we had not done anything spiritually. I replied to him that Rosemary and I, along with our five children, had been going to the hospital, gathering around his bed, laying hands on him as described in the Scriptures that Christians should do and had been praying for him.

My brother asked me if I would pray like that for Dad in front of the rest of the family, to which I replied, "Yes."

Dad came home from hospital for the weekend to see if he could cope. On Saturday night, the whole family gathered with all the children and grandchildren there.

After dinner, my brother Gary called all the family together into our kitchen, the traditional gathering place of our family, and explained that Rosemary, our five children and I had been going to the hospital and gathering around his bed and praying for Dad. He said to everyone, "And Bruce has said he will do it front of all of us now."

I will never forget the way he looked at me and pointed at me and said, "Do it, do it now. Go on, do it."

Have you ever had those moments when life seems to be in slow motion?

As I looked around the kitchen, everybody wanted Dad to live.

Our father was an amazing man. In our minds, he was a great man. He had truly sacrificed his life for his five sons and Mum, whom he loved passionately. Dad was smart, wise and strong. He wasn't perfect, but that made him all the greater in our minds…and who is perfect, anyway? Dad was the person you went to for conversation and advice when you needed wisdom. Dad was the person whose affirmation you sought because of who he was.

Across the kitchen was Mum. This had all happened so suddenly.

As I looked at my family that I love and whose pain was so evident, I heard the gentle whisper of the Holy Spirit say, "What is God's will?"

I said to everyone that we could pray for two things right now, "God, please let Dad live," or "God your perfect will be done."

I know what I wanted, and so we gathered around him with great emotion and laid hands on him as a family, and we prayed.

Three weeks later, Dad died.

✦

Let me say it again, you are holding a book that is about praying for others that you love, so why did I start by talking about you being a person of prayer and experiencing a conversion of heart?

Prayer leads us to a conversion of the heart, where we begin to see things with God's eyes.

God allows things to happen that he uses for a much greater good in our lives and in the world:

We know that all things work together for good for those who love God, who are called according to his purpose.

Romans 8:28

Some of the most devastating and heart-breaking circumstances in my life have led to opportunities that would never have come about if I had got my way in prayer. I am so pleased and thank God that He has said no to me at times. I only see certain things and understand certain things, but God sees everything, comprehends all things and sees what will come about in the long run.

Besides all this, God sees both our human life and the eternal Life. He sees all, and so His wisdom and compassion is boundless.

This is not to say that sometimes we pray and pray and our prayers are not answered, and that can be heartbreaking.

For my thoughts are not your thoughts, nor are your ways my ways, says the Lord.

For as the heavens are higher than the earth, so are my ways higher than your ways and my thoughts than your thoughts.
Isaiah 55:8–9

BALANCING THE ASK AND FAITH

It is from this place of the conversion of our heart that we can bring our needs to God because the way we see with the 'eyes of our converted heart' will now be different. It will affect the way we pray for those we love because we will be asking for God's perfect will to be done.

The Scriptures teach us, but prayer enables us to hold in tension the need as Jesus says, to place our needs before God and ask very specific prayers but at the same time trust that God would do his perfect will in the situation.

This is the place of the conversion of our heart.

Praying for Someone You Love will bless you as well as the people you pray for.

PART 2:
WHO AM I
PRAYING FOR

On this page, you can write the name or names of people you are praying for, including yourself. You can also write down what you are specifically praying for each of them. Be careful, however, what you write, as others may read this. Private information should not be written here.

1. _____

2. _____

3. _____

4. _____

5. _____

6. _____

7. _____

8. _____

9. _____

10. _____

11. _____

12. _____

13. _____

14. _____

15. _____

16. _____

17. _____

18. _____

19. _____

20. _____

21. _____

22. _____

23. _____

24. _____

25. _____

26. _____

27. _____

28. _____

29. _____

30. _____

31. _____

32. _____

33. _____

34. _____

35. _____

36. _____

PART 3: SCRIPTURE TO HELP US PRAY

The Scriptures are God's inspired word to us both as the Church and as individuals. It is important to reflect upon it and allow it to speak to our heart.

When you read the following passage, find a place where you can write some notes. You will be amazed by what you will see and experience as the Word of God comes alive.

Asks yourself these FIVE questions in this order.

1. What do you see?

2. What do you think it means?

3. What do you think God is saying to you about it?

4. What are you going to do about it?

5. What are you going to pray about it?

Day 1 John 9:1-12

A Man Born Blind Receives Sight

Day 2 Luke 7:1-10

Jesus Heals a Centurion's Servant

Day 3 Luke 7:36-50

A Sinful Woman Forgiven

Day 4 Matthew 7:7-11

Ask, Search, Knock

Day 5 Matthew 6:25-34

Do Not Worry

Day 6 Matthew 6:5-14

Concerning Prayer

Day 7 Mark 7:31-37

Jesus Cures a Deaf Man

Day 8 Mark 8:22-26

Jesus Cures a Blind Man

Day 9 Luke 2:41-52

The Boy Jesus in the Temple

Day 10 Luke 5:33-39

The Question About Fasting

Day 11 John 2:1-12

The Wedding at Cana

Day 12 Luke 8:22-25

Jesus Calms a Storm

Day 13 Mark 11:20-25

The Lesson from the Withered Tree

Day 14 Matthew 14:22-33

Jesus Walks on water

Day 15 Matthew 18:21-35

Forgiveness

Day 16 Matthew 22:34-40

The Greatest Commandment

Day 17 Mark 6:30-44

Feeding the Five Thousand

Day 18 Mark 8:14-21

The Yeast of the Pharisees

Day 19 Luke 4:1-13

The Temptation of Jesus

Day 20 Luke 5:17-26

Jesus Heals a Paralytic

Day 21 Luke 6:37-42

Judging Others

Day 22 Mark 10:35-45

The Request of James and John

Day 23 John 8:1-11

The Woman Caught in Adultery

Day 24 John 13:1-20

Jesus Washes the Disciples' Feet

Day 25 Luke 18:18-30

The Rich Ruler

Day 26 Luke 19:11-27

The Parable of the Ten Pounds

Day 27 Luke 17:11-19

Jesus Cleanses Ten Lepers

Day 28 Matthew 16:13-20

Peter's Declaration about Jesus

Day 29 Matthew 26:36-46

Jesus Prays in Gethsemane

Day 30 John 21:1-14

Jesus Appears to the Disciples

Day 31 John 21:15-19

Jesus and Peter

PART 4: A DAILY QUOTE FROM THE SAINTS

Day 1   He who labors as he prays lifts his heart to God with his hands.

St Benedict of Nursia

Day 2   When you lie down on your bed, remember with thanksgiving the blessings and the providence of God.

St Antony the Great

Day 3 He did not say: You will not be troubled – you will not be tempted – you will not be distressed. But He said: You will not be overcome.

St Julian of Norwich

Day 4 One must not think that a person who is suffering is not praying. He is offering up his sufferings to God and many a time he is praying much more truly than the one who goes away by himself and meditates his head off, and, if he has squeezed out a few tears, thinks that is prayer.

St Teresa of Avila

Day 5 If we can enter the church day and night and implore God to hear our prayers, how careful we should be to hear and grant the petitions of our neighbours in need.

St Francis of Assisi

Day 6 When someone said to him "I don't believe in God," he smiled and replied: but God believes in you.

St Padre Pio

Day 7 Let nothing disturb you, nothing frighten you: all things are passing, God never changes.

St Teresa of Avila

Day 8 Contemplation is nothing else than a secret, peaceful and loving infusion of God, which if admitted, will set the soul on fire with the Spirit of Love.

St John of the Cross

Day 9 God dwells within you, and there you should dwell with Him.

St Teresa of Avila

Day 10 It is our part to seek, His to grant what we ask; ours to make a beginning, His to bring it to completion; ours to offer what we can, His to finish what we cannot.

St Jerome

Day 11 It is simply impossible to lead, without prayer, a virtuous life.

St John Chrysotom

Day 12 Prayer is a deep conversation, which takes place when we exchange not only words, but our thoughts, hearts, feelings, in other words when we give of our own selves.

St John Paul II

Day 13 Prayer is nothing else than being on a friendship basis with Christ.

St Teresa of Avila

Day 14 Everyone of us needs a half an hour of prayer every day then when we are busy- we need an hour.

St Francis de Sales

Day 15 The fruit of silence is prayer, the fruit of prayer is faith, the fruit of faith is love, the fruit of love is service, the fruit of service is peace.

St Teresa of Calcutta

Day 16 Pray, hope and don't worry. Worry is useless. God is merciful and will hear your prayer.

St Padre Pio

Day 17 Patience, Prayer and Silence. These are what gives strength to the soul.

St Faustina

Day 18 Prayer is in fact a recognition of our limits, and our dependence: we come from God, we are of God and to God we will return.

St John Paul II

Day 19 He who avoids prayer, avoids everything that is good.

St John of the Cross

Day 20 I used to believe that prayer changes things, but now I know that prayer changes us, and we change things.

St Teresa of Calcutta

Day 21 Prayer is the place of refuge for every worry, a foundation for cheerfulness, a source of constant happiness, a protection against sadness.

St John Crystotrom

Day 22 The highest form of prayer is to stand silently in awe before God.

St Isaac the Syrian

Day 23 Prayer is to our Soul what rain is to the soil. Fertilize the soil every so richly, it will remain barren, unless feed by frequent rains.

St John Vianney

Day 24 Don't worry to the point of losing your inner peace. Pray with perserverance, calmness and serenity.

St Padre Pio

Day 25 He who prays most receives most.

St Alphonsus Ligurio

Day 26 And every day, especially when your heart feels the loneliness of life: pray.

St Padre Pio

Day 27 When you say the Our Father, Gods ear is next to your lips.

St Andre Bessette

Day 28 When we pray the voice of our heart must be heard more than the proceedings from the mouth.

St Bonaventure

Day 29 Pain, suffering and sorrow are but the kiss of Jesus. A sign that you have come so close to him that he has kissed you.

St Teresa of Calcutta

Day 30 Arm yourself with prayer rather than a sword, adorn yourself with humility rather than fine clothes.

St Dominic

Day 31 Prayer is an act of Love, words are not needed. Even if sickness distracts our thoughts, all that is needed is the will to Love.

St Teresa of Avila

PART 5: PRAYERS OLD AND NEW

Do you ever feel lost as to what to say to God? I know I have at times. Often the prayers of others can be very helpful in our relationship with God.

I encourage you to carry this book and choose prayers appropriate to where you are and what you are praying about.

They include prayers that are Christian for everyone and are followed by specifically Catholic prayers. My prayer for you is that these will help in your relationship with God.

THE CATHOLIC GUY RULE OF LIFE DAILY PRAYER

A member of The Catholic Guy Community commits to praying at least five times a day with the entire Community and Ministry.

The Catholic Guy Rule of Life Prayer;

- Is a reminder of who we are.

- Draws us deeper into God.

- Helps us become who we are called to be.

First in the Morning

Lord Jesus use me and every member of our Church community to bring your presence into the lives of all people we meet today.

Meals & at the beginning of Meetings

Lord Jesus give me and every member of our Church community a hunger today to see all people encounter you as their personal Lord and Saviour.

Last at Night

Lord Jesus thank you that you have used me and our Church community to be your presence in the lives of all those we met today.

The Catholic Guy Prayer of
Commitment of Our Life to God

Lord Jesus, I want to belong to you from now.
I want to give my whole self to you.
I ask your forgiveness for all the sins and
failings in my life.
I want to carry you in my heart just as you
hold me precious in your heart.
Lord, I give myself to you.
Amen.

PRAYERS FOR
INTENTIONS AND NEEDS

At this Moment

At this moment I'm far from happy about
my situation.
There's so much unfinished business...
There are decisions I've been putting off and
words that need to be said...
There are things and people in the past that
I still haven't let go...
There are memories of hurt done to me and
done by me...
And memories of joy I've yet to celebrate...
At this moment, I feel imprisoned, like a
printed word.

Locked in a space that denies me freedom to reach out for healing, to move on with hope, to love with all my heart. Lord, comfort and cheer your servant who, at this moment, feels quite low. Amen.

Blessed be God

Blessed are you, O God, you are good and great.

Beyond our ability to imagine you have filled us with joy.

Even though things did not turn out as we expected, we should have realised that you would not let us down.

Blessed are you for your compassion that feels the pain in the hearts of those you love and pours the calming oil of mercy on the anxious and worried.

Keep us in your company, and keep the ones we pray for safe from harm.

Bring their lives to fulfillment in happiness and enrich us all with your peace. Amen.

Abandonment

Father, I abandon myself into Your hands. Do with me whatever You will. Whatever You may do, I thank You. I am ready for all,

I accept all. Let only Your will be done in me, and in all Your creatures. I wish no more than this, O Lord. Into Your hands, I commend my spirit; I offer it to You, Lord, and so need to give myself, to surrender myself into Your hands, without reserve and with boundless confidence, for You are my Father. Amen.

Addiction

Lord Jesus, You said, "I have come to set the captives free." We are captive and need your healing touch. Free us, Lord, from our addictions, so that we will be:

Free from the cares and worries that stifle our happiness;

Free from sins that cling to us, and to which we cling;

Free from all compulsive behavior that prevents us from becoming what you, Lord, have planned for us. Bring us, loving Savior, to the experience of abundant life, which you promised. Amen.

Adversity

Today I want to thank You, Lord, for adversity.

I am so grateful for all that I have been through.

Yes, at times I thought it was too much.

At times I was even mad at You, God.

I didn't understand why I had to go through it.

It felt like too much. It didn't feel fair, yet there You were.

Thank You, Lord, that all that I have been through has made me wonderfully in Your eyes.

Thank You that now I am stronger, built more firmly and established more solidly in Your will.

Lord, thank You for never leaving me! Thank You for always saving me.

Thank You for always helping me. Thank You for always rescuing me.

Thank You for providing me with a way out. When it was darkest, Your light shined through.

When it hurt the most, Your love reached me. When I was the most confused and lost in this world, Your Truth gathered me back into Your arms. When I didn't think it was possible to go on, You showed me I was already in Your Arms.

When I didn't know where to go, You lit a path for my feet.

When I didn't know what to think, You spoke to me.

When I didn't know if it was You, You spoke again and I knew.

Thank You for reaching so far down, to lift me up.

Thank You for showing me that as far down as I was, that is how high I can climb!

Thank You, Lord, that all of my suffering has meaning. Amen.

Affirmation

I am loved by God;

I am made by God;

I am forgiven by God;

I am accepted by God unconditionally;

I am a child of God;

I am sustained by God;

I am important to God;

I am used by God;

I am enabled by God;

I am destined for God. Amen.

Before Starting on a Journey

My holy Angel Guardian, ask the Lord to bless the journey which I undertake, that it may profit the health of my soul and body; that I may reach its end, and that, returning safe and sound, I may find my family in good health. Guard, guide and preserve us. Amen.

Child-Like Faith

Lord, thank You for all the Bible stories about child like faith and wonder.

Lord, I realize how important this is as I get older.

I see how life has a way of hurting me and making me less sensitive.

Lord, today I pray that You renew in me this child like faith and awe.

I want to see with new eyes how amazing Your creation is and how much I mean to You.

Renew my spirit, Lord, that I may be a new creation in You.

Lord, help me to see how dependent children are on their parents, to remind me how dependent I am on You.

The reality is that You are my provider, God.

Let me not forget this as I get ahead in life and am able to provide things that take care of my worldly needs.

Lord, don't ever let me become too self-sufficient to where I have an ego.

Lord, I pray that You fill me with that child-like wonder, that I may be inspired a fresh.

Renew me today, Lord. Amen.

Choosing a State of Life

From all eternity, O Lord, You planned my very existence and my destiny. You wrapped me in Your love in baptism and gave me the Faith to lead me to an eternal life of happiness with You. You have showered me with Your graces, and You have been always ready with Your mercy and forgiveness when I have fallen. Now I beg You for the light I so earnestly need that I may find the way of life in which lies the best fulfillment of Your will. Whatever state this may be, give me the grace necessary to embrace it with love of Your holy will as devotedly as Your Blessed Mother did Your will. I offer myself to You now, trusting in Your wisdom and love to direct me in working out my salvation and in helping others to know and come close to

You, so that I may find my reward in union with You for ever and ever. Amen.

Confirmation

Lord, God Almighty, I thank you for protecting me from every form of evil and bringing me the gift of your divine health. I thank you for breaking the chains of oppression and delivering me from every form of sin, sickness, disease and lie of the enemy. I thank you for the powerful name of Jesus to which every knee shall bow.

In the power and authority that you have given me, I say to all addictions, perversions, chemical dependencies, hopelessness, worry, doubt, fear, despair and all symptoms of any such illness that you must submit to the name of Jesus. I cast down every argument and proud obstacle that exalts itself against the knowledge of God. I bring every thought captive to the obedience of Christ.

Thank you for giving me your authority over all the power of the enemy. Nothing shall harm me. I call upon a heavenly spirit of praise and worship to fill and guard me against the enemy's lies. Thank you for your full armor, your name, your most precious blood and your Holy Spirit. No weapon formed against me shall prosper. Thank you, heavenly Father, for all your provisions, for yours is the kingdom, the power and the glory, both now and forevermore. Amen.

Dignity of Human Life

Lord and giver of all life, help us to value each person, created in love by you.
In your mercy, guide and assist our efforts to promote the dignity and value of all human life, born and unborn. We ask this through Christ our Lord. Amen.

Employment

God, our Father, I turn to you seeking your divine help and guidance as I look for suitable employment. I need your wisdom to guide my footsteps along the right path and to lead me to find the proper things to say and do in this quest. I wish to use the gifts and talents you have given me, but I need the opportunity to do so with gainful employment. Do not abandon me, dear Father, in this search, but rather grant me this favor I seek so that I may return to you with praise and thanksgiving for your gracious assistance. Grant this through Christ, our Lord. Amen.

Employment

Bless, O Lord of the centuries and the millennia, the daily work by which men and women provide bread for themselves and their loved ones. We also offer to your fatherly hands the toil and sacrifices associated with work, in union with your Son Jesus Christ, who redeemed human work from the yoke of sin and restored it to its original dignity. Amen.

Pope John Paul II

Faithfulness

Lord, I am so very thankful for Your faithfulness and loving kindness.

You never change, You never fail, You never turn from me.

Lord, it is I who am unfaithful, and I am the one who turns away.

Yet You accept me with open arms and even more love when I snap out of it and run back to You. Lord, today I raise my hands to You afresh.

Today I am pointing to You for all to see that You are the Holy one.

Lord, people let me down. They fail me all the time. They make promises they don't keep.

Help me to forgive them as You forgive me. Help me to see that is why I need You.

Your Truth and Faithfulness never end. Help me to abide in You, Lord.

Lord, just as a picture I take can be blurry, yet come in clearer as it develops, develop my faithfulness to You. Help me to understand what I need to do, Lord.

Build in me a trust that if I don't understand it, I just have to trust in You.

Lord, the economy changes. The fashions change.

What is popular today changes so fast that it proves to me that it is all an illusion. It is all a distraction.

Thank You for showing this to me and building in me a firm foundation in You.

You never change, You never fail, You always forgive me when I turn in repentance.

You are my God, and I thank You. Amen.

Forgiveness

O God, mercy and forgiveness are Yours by nature and by right. Receive our humble petitions. Though we are bound tightly by the chain of our sins, set us free by the power of Your great mercy. Amen.

Gift of Giving

Today I want to thank You, Lord, for the gift of giving.

Thank You for showing me that it is better to give than receive.

Lord, thank You that the more I give, the bigger and more open my heart gets for You to enter.

Thank You, Lord, that giving doesn't have to be in a monetary value, it can be my time and energy. Thank You that even when I don't have much money, even my small donations enhance Your kingdom.

Thank You for being able to take the smallest amount, to feed many.

Thank You for letting me spread Your love and fragrance everywhere I go.

Flood my soul with Your Spirit and love.

Penetrate me so deeply that my life comes from Your radiance.

Make me glow of You that I can be a blessing to others.

Lead me to where I can use what You have given me to help others.

Shine a light where You want me to go.

Open doors that You want me to enter.

Lord, remind me that all that I have is a gift from You and I am only borrowing it.

Remind me that I can't out give You.

Thank You for all that You give me every day. Amen.

Guidance and Direction

Lord, today I want to thank You for the guidance and direction You give me through the Holy Spirit.

When Jesus ascended to be with the Father in heaven, the Holy Spirit came down to live in all of us.

I thank You that as the Son of God, Jesus lived through all of our trials and was tempted in every way. Because of this, the Holy Spirit is our guide.

Sometimes I wander off the path and start doing what I think is best without praying about it.

Please forgive me from making decisions apart from You.

Give me the strength to change and plant You at the center of all that I do.

Thank You, Lord, that I know I have the Holy Spirit burning in me.

Thank You that I know that my excitement and inspiration comes from You.

I love to feel Your warm embrace when I do things that make You very happy.

Thank You for nudging me and pushing me to make hard choices that I know are Biblical and right, even when I don't want to.

Thank You for speaking to me Your word. Amen.

Guidance and Grace

Oh my God, You know my weaknesses and failings, and that without Your help I can accomplish nothing for the good of souls, my own and others. Grant me, therefore, the help of Your grace. Grant it according to my particular needs this day. Enable me to see the task You will set before me in the daily routine of my life, and help me work hard at my appointed tasks. Teach me to bear patiently all the trials of suffering or failure that may come to me today. Amen.

Gratitude

Lord God, may we be grateful for our lot, and compassionate toward all those who are suffering every kind of distress at this difficult time.

May we hold back nothing, and hasten to be the ministers of prayer and mercy, like the disciples of Him who went about doing good in times of need. Amen

Prayer for Guidance and Help

Dear Lord, I am calling upon you today for your divine guidance and help. I am in crisis and need a supporting hand to keep me on the right and just path.

My heart is troubled, but I will strive to keep it set on you, as your infinite wisdom will show me the right way to a just and right resolution. Thank you for hearing my prayer and for staying by my side. Amen.

Hope

Lord, I want to thank You for the Hope I have in You.

Thank You for knowing me so well that every tear I shed is counted.

This life is not all there is and for that I thank You.

Many people are living for this life and all that they can get out of it, and for them I pray You intervene and give them the same chance You have given me.

Lord, even when the days are hard and I feel overwhelmed,

there You are breathing fresh hope into me.

In hope, I expectantly wait with faith that You are my shield of salvation.

In hope, I know You are for me and that nothing can stand against me.

In hope, I know that even if You rescue me in the very last second it is for my good, so I know it is indeed You who has moved.

Thank You, Lord, for guiding me into Your will so that I may hope for things You want me to have and not for selfish things that aren't in Your will.

Thank You that it is okay to hope for my marriage to be overflowing with love, for prosperity and joy. Thank You that I have the hope of seeing You in heaven where the streets are lined with gold.

Thank You that when times get tough down here, that by holding on to Your hope, I can make heaven out of a bad situation anyway. Amen.

Hope

Heavenly Father, I am your humble servant, I come before you today in need of hope. There are times when I feel helpless, there are times when I feel weak. I pray for hope. I need hope for a better future. I need hope for a better life. I need hope for love and kindness.

Some say that the sky is at its darkest just before the light. I pray that this is true, for all seems dark. I need your light, Lord, in every way.

I pray to be filled with your light from head to toe. To bask in your glory. To know that all is right in the world, as you have planned, and as you want it to be.

Help me to walk in your light, and live my life in faith and glory. In your name I pray, Amen.

Inspiration

Lord, today I want to thank You for inspiration.

You are the Master Painter who created all things.

You have breathed life into us and also blessed us with special gifts.

Inspiration is one of those awesome gifts You have given us.

Thank You for all those times when You planted a thought in my head to do something good for someone.

Thank You for how close I felt to You for doing it and seeing that person blessed by it.

Thank You for the inspiration to create things, make things beautiful, design things and find ways to do my job better.

Thank You for the inspiration to be a better husband, wife, father, brother, sister, son, member of my church, member of my community and employee.

Lord, thank You that today is a new day, full of new inspiration.

I have faith that You can help me invent something amazing today, write something profound, start a business that succeeds, or do something even more powerful – find a way to bring someone to You.

I pray that You pour out this inspiration to overflowing today.
Pour so much out that I can't contain it all.
Amen.

In Times of Confusion and Hurt

I'm hurting, Lord. I admit it.
I'm scared and confused.
So, I'm asking you to remember,
to remember all those promises
you give in your Word.
Help me to remember those promises.
I'm relying on them.
They've given me hope in the past,
and I need to hold tight to them now.
They will revive and comfort me.
I know you won't forget me, Jesus.
I remember with you there's hope -
not a wishful hope – a certain hope.
Hope for the here and now.
Hope for my future.
Hope as I face this challenge,
leaning on you and your promises. Amen.

In Time of Need

Heavenly Father, in my present need, help me to believe that You are aware of my anxiety and will do what is best for me. Give me the strength to trust You and put the present and future in Your hands. Grant this through Christ our Lord. Amen.

Overcoming Life's Hardships

O Lord, we call upon You in our time of sorrow, That You give us the strength and will to bear our heavy burdens, until we can again feel the warmth and love of Your divine compassion. Be mindful of us and have mercy on us while we struggle to comprehend life's hardships.

Keep us ever in Your watch, until we can walk again with light hearts and renewed spirits. Amen.

Patience

Sit with me awhile, Lord, and keep me sitting. Don't let me rush around frantically active but getting nowhere.

Look me in the eye, Lord, stare me out.

Keep me still long enough to know that hearts still beat and life goes on without my constant monitoring.

Come into my life, Lord, and help me see your purpose.

Not a wild parade, wanting everything done yesterday, demanding perfection and precision.
But a quiet collaboration with the Maker of it all.
Letting everything unfold in grateful wonder at such patient love. Amen.

Peaceful Rest

Dear Lord Jesus, as I rest in the comfort of your love, I ask to experience your gentle embrace as you tenderly wrap your loving arms around me. I trust your compassionate care will bring peace to my mind, serenity to my heart and renewal to my spirit.

In your loving embrace, I ask that you grant me a peaceful night's rest. Please purify my dreams, cleanse my subconscious and wash my thoughts with the purity of your infinite love. Please minister to my heart, mind, body, soul and spirit as I rest in your compassionate care tonight.

Please send forth your protective angels to stand guard over me as I sleep. May your angelic army destroy all curses, hindrances and demonic influences that have been sent against my ability to experience a peaceful night's rest. I ask that your heavenly host protect me as I stay awake and watch over me as I sleep, that awake I may keep watch with Christ, and asleep, rest in his peace. Amen.

Personal Forgiveness

Lord Jesus, I am sorry for my sins, I renounce Satan and all his works, and I give you my life. I accept you, whom I've just received in communion. I now receive and accept you as my personal Lord and my personal Savior, and as we just prayed, fill us with Your Holy Spirit. Amen.

Pornography

Dear Lord, give me the strength and sense to keep from visiting internet sites or otherwise looking at salacious materials that will only entice me further into a slime pit of sin and shame. Let me remember that such sites and magazines, however appealing at first, can become dangerously addictive with images that cloud my mind and turn me away from the true value of sexuality in loving my spouse. Shield me from wishing to partake of the poison of pornography, whether soft or hard, remembering that however sweet it may taste at first, it can all too quickly turn quite bitter, leaving me obsessing over base desires and my spouse feeling threatened and abandoned. Blessed Mother Mary, I ask for your help and grace in these matters as well, in the name of Your Beloved Son, Christ our Lord. Amen.

Prosper in School and Work

Dear God the Father, I praise and glorify you. I pray that You help me in my studies. I know that You want me, Your child, to prosper in all my endeavours.

Give me Your knowledge and wisdom as I study for my lessons and exams. Let me learn my lessons properly and understand them completely. I pray that I overcome all my academic weaknesses. Take control of my thoughts.

Bless me with this, O Lord, for your greater glory. Let me be a blessing to my family that I love so much. I thank You in advance for answering my prayer.

In Jesus' name, I pray. Amen.

Prosper in New Job

My Loving Father, I cast all my worries upon You. I have so much anxiety and fear in my heart about this new job I have. Fill my heart with desire to do great things and bless the work of my hands. I completely trust You and have deep faith in You.

Let all that I do be pleasing to you. Grant me wisdom and knowledge that I may do what is good and true in all the days of my life. Let me feel Your mighty presence, dear God, as I give You my praise and thanks. Amen.

Protection of Life

Loving God, I thank you for the gift of life you gave and continue to give to me and to all of us.

Merciful God, I ask your pardon and forgiveness for my own failure and the failure of all people to respect and foster all forms of life in our universe.

Gracious God, I pray that with your grace, I and all people will reverence, protect, and promote all life and that we will be especially sensitive to the life of the unborn, the abused, neglected, disabled, and the elderly. I pray, too, that all who make decisions about life in any form will do so with wisdom, love, and courage.

Living God, I praise and glorify you as Father, Source of all life, as Son, Savior of our lives, and as Spirit, Sanctifier of our lives. Amen.

Reflection

I asked God for strength, that I might achieve;
I was made weak, that I might learn humbly to obey.
I asked for health, that I might do great things;
I was given sickness, that I might do better things.
I asked for riches, that I might be happy;
I was given poverty, that I might be wise.
I asked for power to have the praise of others;
I was given weakness, to feel the need for God.
I asked for all things, that I might enjoy life;
I was given life, that I might enjoy all things.
I receive nothing I asked for – but everything I hoped for.

Almost despite myself, my unspoken prayer
was answered;
I am, among all people, most richly blessed.
Amen.

Remembering our Dead

God of all consolation, in Jesus your Son,
our Saviour and Brother, you accompany us
as we journey to you.
You shelter us in the shade of your out-
stretched arm.
You give light in our darkness, and guide us
beside crystal streams.
You are with us in life and in death.
Though death separates us from those we
love, Your presence is the bridge that carries
our hope.
Keep watch, that all your people, in life or in
death might remain in your love, and rest in
your peace. Amen.

Serenity Prayer

O God, grant me to accept the things I can-
not change, courage to change the things
I can, and wisdom to know the difference.
Amen.

Sorrow

God of all consolation, in Your unending love and mercy for us, You turn the darkness of death into the dawn of new life. Show compassion to Your people in sorrow. Be our refuge and our strength to lift us from the darkness of this grief to peace and joy in Your presence. We ask this through Christ our Lord. Amen.

Spiritual Gifts

Lord, today I want to thank You for the spiritual gifts You have given me.
You have given me countless opportunities and gifts that are suited to me in this life.
Thank You for giving me the Holy Spirit to live inside of me.
Thank You for making me a son of God.
Lord, I thank You for all the spiritual gifts I see in believers all around me.
Thank You for the gift of prophecy, thank You for the gift of service, thank You for the gift of teaching, thank You for the gift of exhortation, thank You for the gift of giving, thank You for the gift of leadership, thank You for the gift of mercy, thank You for the gift of wisdom, thank You for the gift of

knowledge, thank You for the gift of faith, thank You for the gift of healing, thank You for the gift of miracles, thank You for the gift of discerning what is of You and what is not of You, and thank You for the gift of worshipping You.

Lord, today let me see how all these gifts are parts of one body.

Lord, let me see where I fit into this kingdom that I may become fastened securely into place where You want me to be. Amen.

Strength

Lord, give me strength today to be firmly established in Your will for me.

If I feel weak and fragile today, provide Your strength and fortitude.

Lord, when I am weak, You are strong.

Just as my computer or cell phone needs to be recharged often,

I need to be plugged in to You as well.

I thank You that it can be as simple as saying two words, "God, help."

You never let me down, You never turn away. The only one who turns away is me and I am thankful to You that I know that is when I'm in trouble. All I have to do is turn toward

You and talk to You or sing to You, and I am recharged with Your strength physically, emotionally and spiritually.

Break through my day often with little reminders of Your presence and love.

Lord, when I'm separated from You by my thoughts, I am in trouble.

Keep me close to You and thirsty for Your goodness, and I won't grow weary.

Thank you for giving me the strength to face whatever comes my way today. Amen.

Strength and Courage

Lord, you are Holy above all others, and all the strength that I need is in your hands.

I am not asking, Lord, that you take this trial away. Instead, I simply ask that Your will be done in my life. Whatever that means, that is what I want.

But I admit that it's hard, Lord.

Sometimes I feel like I can't go on. The pain and the fear are too much for me, and I know that I don't have the strength on my own to get through this.

I know that I can come to you, Jesus, and that you will hear my prayer. I know that it is not your intent to bring me to this point just to leave me in the wilderness alone.

Please, Lord, give me the strength that I need to face today. I don't have to worry about tomorrow.

If you just give me the strength that I need today, that is all I need.

Keep me from sinning during this trial. Instead, help me to keep my eyes on you. You are the Holy Lord, and all of my hope rests in you.

Thank you for hearing my prayer. In Jesus' name. Amen.

Strength and Wisdom

Thank you, Lord, for being there for me and allowing me to cry out to you in my times of need.

It is amazing to me that the Lord of the Universe would take time to listen to me and to care about what I say.

God, there are things happening around me right now that I do not understand. Some of these things make me feel weak, helpless and afraid.

Even in the midst of this, I know that you are the Lord.

I know that the situation is in Your hand, and I trust You.

I beseech you for strength and for wisdom that I would be able to endure this situation and be able to handle it in a way that would bring glory to Your name.

In Jesus name. Amen

Strength for a Friend

Lord, I come before you today knowing that all power is in Your hand. I know that you are the Lord and that you care for your people. Right now, my friend is struggling with a difficult trial. I can see her strength is faltering, Lord, and I know that you have all of the strength that she needs.

I pray that you will reach down and touch her right now wherever she is at this moment. Let your presence fill the room where she is and let her feel an extra portion of your strength that can help her to get through this day.

She needs you now, Lord, and I thank you in advance for meeting her where she is and shoring up her strength during this difficult time. In Jesus' name. Amen.

Success in Work

Glorious Saint Joseph, model of all those who are devoted to labor, obtain for me the grace to work conscientiously, putting the call of duty above my many sins; to work with thankfulness and joy, considering it an honor to employ and develop, by means of labor, the gifts received from God; to work with order, peace, prudence and patience, never surrendering to weariness or difficulties; to work, above all, with purity of intention, and with detachment from self, having always death before my eyes and the account which I must render of time lost, of talents wasted, of good omitted, of vain complacency in success so fatal to the work of God. All for Jesus, all for Mary, all after thy example, O Patriarch Joseph. Such shall be my motto in life and death. Amen.

Suffering

Behold me, my beloved Jesus, weighed down under the burden of my trials and sufferings, I cast myself at Your feet, that You may renew my strength and my courage, while I rest here in Your presence. Permit me to lay down my cross in Your Sacred Heart, for only Your infinite goodness can sustain me; only Your love can help me bear my cross; only Your powerful hand can lighten its weight. O Divine King, Jesus, whose heart is so compassionate to the afflicted, I wish to live in You, during my life be to me my model and support; at the hour of my death, be my hope and my refuge. Amen

The Unborn

Heavenly Father, You created us in Your own image, and You desire that not even the least among us should perish. In Your love for us, You entrusted Your only Son to the holy Virgin Mary. Now, in Your love, protect against the wickedness of the devil, those little ones to whom You have given the gift of life. Amen.

Transformation

Dear Heavenly Father,

We love you and lift your name up as our sovereign Lord.

You are God the Father, God the Son and God the Holy Spirit.

We look to you for our salvation, guidance, and protection.

We count on you to pour out blessings
to take care of our needs financially
and emotionally.
Even more important we pray for a closer
relationship with you
that we may also bring that love to our families and our communities.
May your Holy Spirit light a fire inside all of
our souls that brings us closer to You.
May You transform us from the inside out
through Your Word and prayer.
We ask that You conform our minds to what
is pleasing to You.
Give all of us a hunger for a deeper understanding and relationship with You. Amen.

Unfailing Strength

Do not look forward to what may happen
tomorrow; the same everlasting Father who
cares for you today will take care of you tomorrow and every day. Either He will shield
you from suffering, or He will give you unfailing strength to bear it.

Be at peace, then. Put aside all anxious
thoughts and imaginations, and say continually: "The Lord is my strength and my
shield. My heart has trusted in Him and I

am helped. He is not only with me but in me, and I in Him. Amen.

While you are waiting

Jesus, your promise to be always with us is especially real for me right now.

I wait to welcome you as a most honoured guest into my home and into my life.

Thank you for the sacred food by which you come to me and for the nourishment and strength it brings. Thank you, too, for the one who carries you to me.

Keep this servant safe and fill their own needs with your generous love.

May Mary, your mother, keep me company this day and gift me with her gentleness that I may be more worthy to share the fruit of her love. Come, Lord Jesus. Amen.

Worry

Dear God, I feel so anxious about what's going on in my life—and what I'm afraid might happen to me in the future—that I spend a lot of time and energy worrying.

My body is suffering with [mention symptoms like insomnia, headaches, an upset stomach, shortness of breath, a racing heart-beat, etc.]. My mind is suffering with [mention symptoms like nervousness, distraction, irritability, and forgetfulness]. My spirit is suffering with [mention symptoms like discouragement, fear, doubt, and hopelessness]. I don't want to live this way anymore. Please send the miracle I need to find peace in the body, mind, and spirit that you have given me!

My all-knowing Father in heaven, please give me the wisdom to see my concerns from the right perspective so they won't overwhelm me. Remind me often of the truth that you are much greater than any situation that concerns me—so I can entrust any circumstance in my life to you, instead of worrying about it. Please give me the faith I need to believe that and trust you with whatever worries me.

From this day forward, please help me develop the habit of turning my worries into prayers.

Whenever an anxious thought enters my mind, ask my guardian angel to alert me to the need to pray about that thought rather than worrying about it. The more I practice praying instead of worrying, the more I can experience the peace you want to give me. I choose to stop assuming the worst about my future and start expecting the best, because you're at work in my life with your great love and power.

I believe that you will help me manage any situation that worries me. Help me distinguish between what I can control and what I can't – and help me take helpful actions on what I can, and trust you to handle what I can't. As Saint Francis of Assisi famously prayed, «make me an instrument of your peace» in my relationships with other people in every situation I encounter.

Help me adjust my expectations so that I'm not putting pressure on myself unnecessarily, worrying about things that you don't want me to be concerned about—like trying to perfect, presenting an image to others that doesn't reflect who I really am, or trying to get other people to be the way I'd like them to be or do what I'd like them to do. As I let go of unrealistic expectations and accept the way my life really is, you will give me the freedom I need to relax and trust you in deeper ways.

God, please help me find a solution to each real problem that I face and stop worrying about the "What if?" problems that may never happen in my future. Please give me a vision of the peaceful future of hope and joy that you have planned for me. I look forward to that future, because it comes from you, my loving Father. Thank you! Amen.

Work Stress

I can do all things through Christ who strengthens me. Philippians 4:13

Heavenly Father! I thank You for the job You have given me! I consider it as a great gift from You. Yet Lord, You know the stress I am undergoing in my job. Sometimes I feel like just quitting due to the heavy pressures and responsibilities pushed upon me. I seem to have lost all my strength, and I am struggling to cope with the world, Lord! Your word says that You love the prosperity of Your children. So, please be with me and bless all my efforts so that I can excel in my career. Grant me Your grace, which is sufficient to carry me through the most difficult times at my work. Let me find favour in the eyes of my authorities! I plead for Your divine wisdom and strength to tide over the problem that crops up in my job. Keep me in perfect peace, O Lord, so that I may do my work with freedom and bring glory to Your name. I know You will do it because You are the one who relieves me whenever I am in distress. I give You all the glory! In Jesus' name I pray. Amen.

Unemployed

Lord Jesus, my desire to work is itself your gift. You gave me talents so I could shine Your light to others in the world. Send Your Spirit to guide me to work that will provide security and joy, and most of all the ability to serve You in love. Saint Jude, I do not know where I am going—and so I call upon you in my need. Bless my spirit with the determination to press on. Give my heart patience and fortitude. Help me, dear friend, to know that God's plan for me is forged out of love. Amen.

Dear God, you know how much I need a new job—both for the financial income, and the opportunities it would provide to use the talents you›ve given me to help make the world a better place.

You also know, God, how hard I've tried to find a job. But so far, all of the hard work I've done during my job search hasn't led to any job offers. All I've found, despite all the time and energy I've spent looking for employment, is rejection. I'm frustrated, my confidence has been shaken, and I'm worried about my future.

God, please send the miraculous breakthrough I need to get a new job soon! Guide me to opportunities to network with the right people, learn about the right job openings to apply for, and figure out how best to develop my skills so I'll be prepared for my next job. Empower me to perform well at my job interviews. Give me favor with the people who are considering who to hire for any jobs that are good matches for me. Please open doors for me to get a good job offer soon, with the type of work I want to do and the salary and benefits I need.

I believe that there are no limits to what you can do for people who trust you.

Thank you for always providing for my needs. I look forward to walking through the doors you will open for me to start working at a new job. Amen.

BIBLICAL PRAYERS

Canticle of Mary

My soul proclaims your greatness, O my God,
and my spirit has rejoiced in you, my Savior;
For you have regarded me as your holy handmaid;
henceforth all generations shall call me blessed;
For you who are mighty, have done great things for me,
and Holy is your Name;
Your mercy is on those who fear you throughout all generations.
You have showed strength with your arm.
You have scattered the proud in the conceit of their heart.
You have put down the mighty from their seat,
and have lifted up the powerless.
You have filled the hungry with good things,
and have sent the rich away empty.
Remembering your mercy,
You have helped your people Israel –
As you promised Abraham and Sarah.
Mercy to their children forever. Amen.

Canticle of the Three Youths

Bless the Lord, all you works of the Lord;
Praise and exalt him above all forever.
Angels of the Lord, bless the Lord;
You heavens, bless the Lord;
All you waters above the heavens, bless
the Lord.
All you hosts of the Lord; bless the Lord.
Sun and moon, bless the Lord;
Stars of heaven, bless the Lord.
Every shower and dew, bless the Lord;
All you winds, bless the Lord.
Fire and heat, bless the Lord;
Cold and chill, bless the Lord.
Dew and rain, bless the Lord;
Frost and cold, bless the Lord.
Ice and snow, bless the Lord;
Nights and days, bless the Lord.
Light and darkness bless the Lord;
Lightning and clouds, bless the Lord.
Let the earth bless the Lord;
Praise and exalt him above all forever.
Mountains and hills, bless the Lord
Everything growing from the earth, bless
the Lord.
You springs, bless the Lord;
Seas and rivers, bless the Lord.

You dolphins and all water creatures, bless
the Lord;
All you birds of the air, bless the Lord.
All you beasts, wild and tame, bless the Lord;
Praise and exalt him above all forever.
You sons of men, bless the Lord;
O Israel, bless the Lord.
Priests of the Lord, bless the Lord.
Servants of the Lord, bless the Lord.
Spirits and souls of the just, bless the Lord.
Holy men of humble heart, bless the Lord.
Ananias, Azarias, Misael, bless the Lord;
Praise and exalt him above all forever.
Let us bless the Father and the Son and the
Holy Ghost;
Let us praise and exalt God above all forever.
Blessed are you in the firmament of heaven;
Praiseworthy and glorious forever.

Prayer of Praise

Praised be the God and Father of our Lord
Jesus Christ, he who in his great mercy gave
us new birth, a birth unto hope which draws
its life from the resurrection of Jesus Christ
from the dead; a birth to an imperishable
inheritance, incapable of fading or defile-
ment, which is kept in heaven for you who

are guarded with God's power through faith;
a birth to a salvation which stands ready to
be revealed in the last days. Amen.

Prayer of Simeon

Lord, now you let your servant go in peace.
Your word has been fulfilled. My own eyes
have seen the salvation which You have prepared in the sight of every people. A light
to reveal You to the nations and the glory of
Your people Israel. Amen.

Psalm 51:1-12

1 Have mercy on me, O God,
   according to your steadfast love;
   according to your abundant mercy
   blot out my transgressions.
2 Wash me thoroughly from my iniquity,
   and cleanse me from my sin.
3 For I know my transgressions,
   and my sin is ever before me.
4 Against you, you alone, have I sinned,
   and done what is evil in your sight,
   so that you are justified in your sentence
   and blameless when you pass judgment.
5 Indeed, I was born guilty,
   a sinner when my mother conceived me.

6 You desire truth in the inward being;
   therefore teach me wisdom in my
   secret heart.
7 Purge me with hyssop, and I shall be clean;
   wash me, and I shall be whiter than snow.
8 Let me hear joy and gladness;
   let the bones that you have crushed rejoice.
9 Hide your face from my sins,
   and blot out all my iniquities.
10 Create in me a clean heart, O God,
   and put a new and right spirit within me.
11 Do not cast me away from your presence,
   and do not take your holy spirit from me.
12 Restore to me the joy of your salvation,
   and sustain in me a willing spirit.
   Amen

FAMILY PRAYERS

Pope Francis' Prayer to the Holy Family (from Amoris Laetitia)

Jesus, Mary and Joseph,
in you we contemplate
the splendor of true love;
to you we turn with trust.
Holy Family of Nazareth,
grant that our families too

may be places of communion and prayer,
authentic schools of the Gospel
and small domestic churches.
Holy Family of Nazareth,
may families never again experience
violence, rejection and division;
may all who have been hurt or scandalized
find ready comfort and healing.
Holy Family of Nazareth,
make us once more mindful
of the sacredness and inviolability of
the family,
and its beauty in God's plan. Amen.

Family

Lord God, from You every family in heaven and on earth takes its name. Father, You are Love and Life. Through Your Son, Jesus Christ, born of woman, and through the Holy Spirit, fountain of divine charity, grant that every family on earth may become for each successive generation a true shrine of life and love.

Grant that Your grace may guide the thoughts and actions of husbands and wives for the good of their families and of all the families in the world.

Grant that the young may find in the family solid support for their human dignity and for their growth in truth and love.

Grant that love, strengthened by the grace of the sacrament of marriage, may prove mightier than all the weakness and trials through which our families sometimes pass. Through the intercession of the Holy Family of Nazareth, grant that the Church may fruitfully carry out her worldwide mission in the family and through the family. Through Christ our Lord, who is the Way, the Truth and the Life. Amen.

Pope John Paul II

Family Unity

Dear God, thank you for the gift of family that you have given me. You know my heart hurts because of the disharmony in my family. I have lost my peace and my health because of the messy situation in our home. I have no one to turn to but You, Lord. You alone can understand the hearts of Your followers as You have created each and every one of us. Only You can bring the hearts of Your men together. Help me forgive other family members, O Lord. Let my family not defile Your name by this disunity. Help us forgive one another of the mistakes we have done to each other and bring us back together in Your name, Father God.

Fill each one of us with your love and understand so we can fully exalt Your name in glory. I know that you will bring back the peace and unity that was once present in our home. I ask this in the precious name of our Lord and Saviour, Jesus Christ. Amen.

Fathers

Saint Joseph, guardian of Jesus and chaste husband of Mary, you passed your life in loving fulfillment of duty. You supported the holy family of Nazareth with the work of your hands. Kindly protect those who trustingly come to you. You know their aspirations, their hardships, their hopes. They look to you because they know you will understand and protect them. You too knew trial, labor and weariness. But amid the worries of material life your soul was full of deep peace and sang out in true joy through intimacy with God's Son entrusted to you and with Mary, his tender Mother. Assure those you protect that they do not labor alone. Teach

them to find Jesus near them and to watch over him faithfully as you have done. Amen.
Pope John XXIII

Finding a Life Companion

Almighty God, hear this relationship prayer. As You are first in my heavenly heart and mind and spirit, so do I desire a companion for my earthly heart and mind and being. Guide me to the partner You know is perfect for me. Help me walk in faith until that time of our first meeting.

Show me how I can become a partner worthy of love. Then guide me through every stage of our relationship, so that, as we move ever closer to You, we grow closer to each other in Love, in Joy, and in Faith. Thank You God, for hearing my prayer. Amen.

Finding a Life Partner

Heavenly Father, You created this world and all its inhabitants. You found that man is not good to be alone. I pray this to You, O Lord, that I am in need of a partner for my life.

You have showed us in the Bible that finding the right partner made numerous couples live a happy life. Bless me, Father, that I may build a family like theirs. I believe, Lord, that You do not deny Your children their joy and happiness.

I pray that the loneliness in my heart will be gone soon. I pray this to You, O Lord. Amen.

Healing a Relationship

Dear Lord, I offer you this prayer, to help me with my current relationship situation. Please take away all the pain and hurt in my heart. Fill it with love, joy, patience, and understanding.

Bless me and my partner, so that we may never surrender to whatever challenges that come our way. Fill our hearts with love for each other, and may you make each one of us realize each other's worth. Please touch the heart of my partner, fill it with much love for me.

Make our complicated relationship become uncomplicated. I seek for your mercy and blessing that you may allow us to spend the rest of our lives with each other. Please make this feeling mutual for both of us. Lead us not into temptations. Guide us wherever we go. Always put us in each other's heart and mind. Thank you Lord for hearing my prayer. I love you. Amen.

Husband's Prayer

O gracious Father, Maker and Preserver of heaven and earth, who in the beginning did institute matrimony, thereby foreshadowing the mystical union of the Church with our Savior Christ, who, during His ministry upon earth, did honor marriage with His first miracle, help me, I pray Thee, by Thy grace to live in holiness and purity with the wife whom Thou hast given me. Mortify in me all violence of earthly passion, all selfishness and inconsiderateness (here name any besetting sin which may be a hindrance to you), that I may love her as Christ loved His Church, cherish and comfort her as my own body, and have as great care for her happiness as for my own. Grant that we may live in peace, without contention; in unity, without discord. [Give us, O Lord, discreet heart and understanding minds, to bring up our children in Thy faith and fear, that they may be obedient to Thee and to Thy commandments, and to all that Thou requirest of them in their duties towards their parents.]

And give us, O Lord, a sufficiency of those things necessary to maintain ourselves and our family according to that rank and calling wherein Thou hast placed us, without excess or vainglory, in singleness and pureness of heart. Grant this for Jesus Christ's sake, to Whom, with Thee and the Holy Ghost, be all honor and glory, now and forever. Amen.

Marriage

Dear Lord, help me to find someone I can truly love who will love me as well. Someone with whom I can gladly share my thoughts, my feelings, indeed my life! Someone with whom I may raise a family in accordance with your will to share your love and give you Glory. May he [or she] be a vessel of joy in good times and a firm pillar of prudent support in bad. Let neither of us forget that you are there to help us in all cases with your help, guidance, and grace. Let me be discerning and not seek someone solely out of loneliness, but out of love for you and my potential spouse. May this be someone I like as well as love, and may we share a deep bond of trust in each other throughout our married lives, until death do us part.

Don't let carnal or other purely worldly desires cloud my judgment about getting married. Help me to listen to the voice of your Holy Spirit instead in this important matter. Heavenly Father, I ask all these things through Christ our Lord, Amen.

Dear Lord, in this time of great trial in our marriage, let my husband/wife and I not succumb to those forces that would weaken or perhaps even break our bond of love in Holy Matrimony, and our vows to You and each other as well. In this troubled time, let us not forget our vows to be there for each other for worse, as well as better; and in sickness, as well as in health. Be a friend and confidant to keep us attuned to Your wishes and desires for us. Keep me and my spouse from nourishing grudges over disagreements or becoming irritable with each other in our stressful situation. Help us to remember Saint Paul's important advice in his letter to the Ephesians not to let the sun go down with us angry at each other. Through Christ our Lord, Amen.

Dear Lord, let me put on your armor and your shield against the temptations to cheat on my spouse. Even just one such dalliance, however innocuous or justified it may seem, is like a dagger thrust straight into the heart of my marriage and family. Let me be conscious not only of its grave sin as a violation of your law of love, but also of the guilt and shame it entails as well. Let me not risk destroying my spouse's trust in me, ripping apart my family, and possibly losing You forever from mortal sin. Give me strength and wisdom to turn away from evil inclinations against marital fidelity immediately when temptation strikes. Let me have the good sense not to put myself in harm's way through occasions of sin. Blessed Mother Mary, I ask for your help and grace in these matters as well, in the name of Your Beloved Son, Christ our Lord. Amen.

Miracle in Marriage

Dear God, so much has happened (for better and for worse) since I've gotten married. Thank you for always being present with my spouse and me through everything. We need you—the source of all love—to help us fix the damage to our relationship that has been caused by [mention the specific issues here].

Our marriage needs a miracle to right now! I feel hurt and frustrated by what's happened, and I confess that sometimes I doubt that our marriage really can get better. Please send me and my spouse a fresh dose of hope to help us believe that our marriage can improve. Open our hearts to you, each other, and your holy angels, so we can fully receive the blessings you want to send us.

Guide us step-by-step to learn how to change our attitudes and actions with each other so our relationship will become stronger. Empower us through your Spirit to forgive each other for mistakes and to choose each new day to treat each other with love, respect, and kindness.

Rekindle the spark of romantic attraction between us and keep the fire of our sexual relationship burning brightly for each other (and no one else).

Inspire us with fresh ideas to express our love for each other sexually in ways that fulfill both of us. Empower us to avoid temptations to sin in ways that can damage our sexual relationship with each other (like pornography and affairs). Help us focus on each other and maintain a passionate relationship within our marriage.

Give us the wisdom we need to communicate clearly with each other, understand each other, and invest enough time and energy into our marriage consistently despite other demands (like work and parenting), so our emotional connection won›t be neglected. Surround us with some caring and trustworthy people who will encourage and support us as we work to build a better marriage. Help us both to stay focused on you as our top priority each day. Lead us in the same direction together: closer to you!

I believe that you can choose to do anything to improve our marriage if both of us are willing to cooperate with your work. Thank you for answering my prayer; I trust in your complete and unconditional love for both of us and look forward to whatever miracles you may bring into our marriage! Amen.

Miscommunication in a Marriage

Dear Lord, you know what path I am on right now and that I am in agony. I am having disharmony in my married life. You have instituted marriage since You found that it is not good for man to be alone.

I deeply believe that You have given me this person to love and to hold for the rest of my days. The Bible has taught me that a threefold cord is not quickly broken. Come and be with us, Lord, for only You can make two broken hearts understand each other. You are the King of Peace, and I know You can change any sad situation in my life.

Father, I know it is Your will that we should lead a loving and peaceful life with one another. Hear me, dear God, to fill us both with more love and to understand each other better to bring unity to our relationship. Help me become more understand to my partner's needs and feelings.

Grant me wisdom that I may know how to deal with this unlikely situation so I can build a house in Your glory. In Jesus' name I pray, O Lord. Amen.

Motherhood

Good Saint Gerard, powerful intercessor before the throne of God, wonder-worker of our day, I call upon you and seek your aid. You know that our marriage has not as yet been blessed with a child and how much my husband and I desire this gift. Please present our fervent pleas to the Creator of life from whom all parenthood proceeds and beseech Him to bless us with a child whom we may raise as His child and heir of heaven. Amen.

Parents' Prayer for Their Children

O God the Father of mankind, who hast given unto me these my children, and committed them to my charge to bring them up for Thee, and to prepare them for eternal life: help me with Thy heavenly grace, that I may be able to fulfill this most sacred duty and stewardship. Teach me both what to give and what to withhold; when to reprove and when to forbear; make me to be gentle, yet firm; considerate and watchful; and deliver me equally from the weakness of indulgence, and the excess of severity; and grant that, both by word and example, I may be careful to lead them in the ways of wisdom and true piety, so that at last I may, with them, be admitted to the unspeakable joys of our true home in heaven, in the company of the blessed Angels and Saints. Amen.

O Heavenly Father, I commend my children to Thy care. Be Thou their God and Father;

and mercifully supply whatever is lacking in me through frailty or negligence. Strengthen them to overcome the corruptions of the world, whether from within or without; and deliver them from the secret snares of the enemy. Pour Thy grace into their hearts, and strengthen and multiply in them the gifts of Thy Holy Spirit, that they may daily grow in grace and in knowledge of our Lord Jesus Christ; and so, faithfully serving Thee here, may come to rejoice in Thy presence hereafter. Amen.

Relatives who don't have Faith

Merciful Lord, who prayed that there be one flock and one shepherd, I ask the light of faith for those who are related to me and do not know You in Your Eucharistic Presence. Give them the joy of Your protecting presence. Bring them into the one fold, of which You are the Master and Lord. Forgive them their sins and teach them the way of repentance. In the end bring them into the larger circle of Your family, to God our Father, to Mary our Mother, and to You our beloved Brother. Amen.

Spouses for each Other

Lord Jesus, grant that my spouse and I may have a true and understanding love for each other. Grant that we may both be filled with faith and trust. Give us the grace to live with each other in peace and harmony. May we always bear with one another's weakness and grow from each other's failings and grant us patience, kindness, cheerfulness and the spirit of placing the wellbeing of one another ahead of ourselves.

May the love that brought us together grow and mature with each passing year. Bring us both ever closer to You through our love for each other. Let our love grow to perfection. Amen.

To have a Child

Abba Father, thank You for giving me hope and expectation that one day I will conceive and bear my own child. Your ears are not closed to my prayers, and you know the deepest desires and intentions of my heart. I love You, Lord, and it is You who put this longing to be a mother/father and consummate our marriage through the gift of a child. I repent for the many times that

I almost gave up and felt frustrated, lonely, and miserable…for doubting your promises, power, and wisdom in the dark days of our lives. I let go of all the stress, pressures, fears, pains, shame, and grief associated with this yearning to have a child and I put this in Your hands.

I bless You, Lord, for You are in full control and dominion over everything great and small. Nothing is hidden from Your sight, and You have the ability, authority, and majestic power to do what I cannot do for myself, my spouse, and our future and destiny. I completely entrust our lives in Your hands knowing that You know what is best for us. I come to You now reminding You of Your wonderful promises to me and my family. No good thing will You withhold from those whose walk is blameless. Those who put their hope and trust in You will never be put to shame nor disappointed. That if I abide You and Your Words abide in Me, I can ask for whatever I wish and it will be granted to me.

I bless our bodies that we can produce and conceive a child. I bless our sexual and reproductive organs to function to the way God originally intended for them to function. I bless my intimacy and union with my spouse to be clean and pure before the eyes of God and that out of our love for God and love for each other, a child will be formed and this child will bind our love for each other and he/she will be used by God for his kingdom. Thank You, Father God, for giving us your Son, Jesus Christ and the Holy Spirit to save, heal, deliver, and restore us. Jesus Himself was born to an earthly mother and it was such a joy for Mary to conceive and bear Him, the Savior of the world. Grant me this same privilege and joy to conceive and bear a child in Your own perfect time. My sorrows will turn into joy (John 16.20), my wailing into dancing. (Psalm 30.11) This is my prayer for a baby, In Jesus' precious name. Amen.

Father, You know my deep desire for a child. A little one to love and to hold, to care for, to cherish.

Grant that my body may conceive and give birth to a beautiful, healthy baby in Your holy image.

Guide me in all my choices so that this conception, my pregnancy and my baby's birth are in line with Your will.

Heavenly Father and Holy Mother, hear this prayer of my heart, mind and spirit. Amen.

God of Abraham, Isaac, Jacob; God who created the universe and sustains it every moment, we praise you, we thank you and we glorify you.

Lord, you who gave a child to Abraham, we thank you, we praise you. Seeing the tears of Hanna, Lord, you gave her a child. Elizabeth, who was barren in her old age, you blessed her with a child.

You who are the giver of all perfect gifts, we ask you to bless us with wonderful children, who will be your chosen instruments to spread your love. The days/months/years of our sorrow and pain for not having a child, we surrender it to you.

We forgive every person who has insulted us or made fun of us because we were not blessed with a child. Jesus, our Lord and Master, bless whose who have hurt us. Fill them with your Holy Spirit.

Lord, whatever be the obstacle to have a child, let it be taken away from us right now with the power of Your precious blood and precious name.

Praise You, Jesus. Thank You Jesus. Amen

PRAYERS FOR HEALING

After Surgery

Blessed Savior, I thank you that this operation is safely past, and now I rest in your abiding presence, relaxing every tension, releasing every care and anxiety, receiving more and more of your healing life into every part of my being. In moments of pain I turn to you for strength, in times of loneliness I feel your loving nearness. Grant that your life and love and joy may flow through me for the healing of others in your name. Amen.

Before Surgery

Loving Father, I entrust myself to your care this day; guide with wisdom and skill the minds and hands of the medical people who minister in your Name, and grant that every cause of illness be removed, I may be restored to soundness of health and learn to live in more perfect harmony with you and with those around me. Through Jesus Christ. Amen.

Against Disease

Lord, Your scripture says that you heal all diseases and whoever believes in You will not perish but have an everlasting life. Strengthen me, Lord, in this time of illness. Sustain him as he lays sick in his bed. When You were on Earth, you did all things good and healed all kinds of sickness.

You healed those who had diseases. You died and rose for our sins and that we may have eternal life, Lord. I believe in my heart that You are here with us today and that with Your most holy power will remove all sicknesses and evils that roam the earth. Let it be done in Your glory, Lord. We praise and glorify Your name, Amen.

Creative Miracles

God of all creation, you who spoke a simple command and brought forth light from the darkness, I call upon you now to send forth your miracle-working power into every aspect of my being. In the same way that you spoke unto the dust of the ground when you created humankind in your own image, I ask you to send forth your healing power into my body. Send forth your word and command every cell, electrical and chemical impulse, tissue, joint, ligament, organ, gland, muscle, bone and every molecule in my body to come under complete and perfect health, strength, alignment, balance and harmony.

It is through you that I live and move and have my being. With every breath I take, I live under your life-giving grace. I ask you to touch me now with the same miracle-working power that you used when you fashioned me inside my mother's womb. As surely as you have created me in your image and likeness, you can also recreate me now and restore my health.

Please fill me with your healing power. Cast out all that should not be inside of me. I ask you to mend all that is broken, root out every sickness and disease, open all blocked arteries and veins, restore my internal organs, rebuild my damaged tissues, remove all inflammation and cleanse me of all infections, viruses and destructive forms of bacteria.

Let the warmth of your healing love flood my entire being, so that my body will function the way it was created to be, whole and complete, renewed in your perfect health. I ask this through my Lord, Jesus Christ, your Son, who lives and reigns with you and the Holy Spirit, one God, for ever and ever. Amen.

Doctors and Nurses

O merciful Father, who has wonderfully fashioned man in your own image, and has made his body to be a temple of the Holy Spirit, sanctify, we pray you, our doctors and nurses and all those whom you have called to study and practice the arts of healing the sick and the prevention of disease and pain. Strengthen them in body and soul, and bless their work, that they may give comfort to those for whose salvation your Son became Man, lived on this earth, healed the sick, and suffered and died on the Cross. Amen.

For Doctor's Wisdom

Dear Lord, guide my doctor's hands and give him wisdom.
Show him the way and help him to heal me.
I put my faith in you and the medical professionals that you have brought to me. Amen.

Healing

Precious Lord Jesus, you came into the world to heal our infirmities and endure our sufferings. You went about healing all who were sick and bringing comfort to those in pain. By a simple command you rebuked Peter's mother-in-law's fever. You spoke directly to the illness, condemned it for its actions and commanded it to leave her body.

In the same way, Lord, you have called all of your disciples to follow your example. You have given us power over all the works of the enemy and sent us forth to make disciples of all nations. In the healing tradition of the church, and through my obedience to your written Word, I hereby take authority over all forms of sickness and disease that have been attacking my health.

In the name of Jesus, under the power and authority of the Lord God Almighty, I command all forms of demonic illness to leave my body now and go straight to the feet of Jesus Christ. Your assignment and influences are over. I rebuke all pain in the name of Jesus, and I command it to get out of my body right now. I rebuke all spirits of infirmity, nerve disorder, lung disorder, brain disorder, heart disease, AIDS, cancer, hypochondria, fatigue, anorexia, leukemia, arthritis, tumors, abnormal growths, diabetes and all other forms of sickness to leave my body now in the name of Jesus.

Lord Jesus, I thank you for your healing power. I ask you to send forth your ministering, medical and surgical angels, to repair and restore any damage that was caused in my body by the presence of sin, sickness or demonically influenced infirmities. I ask that you send forth your Holy Spirit and fill me with your love, light, peace and joy. Come, Holy Spirit, and transform me into the child of God that you intended me to be. Amen.

Dear Lord Jesus, you went about healing all those who were sick and tormented by unclean spirits. You cleansed the lepers, opened the eyes of the blind and by speaking a simple command, you empowered the crippled to rise up and walk. You sent forth your life-giving power to all those in need, including those you raised from the dead.

O Divine Physician, I come to you now in great need of your intervention. I surrender my life and health into your loving hands. I ask you to send forth your healing power into my heart, mind, body, soul and spirit. Remove from me every lie of the enemy and destroy all the word curses that have been spoken against my health.

If I have accepted medical beliefs that I should not have, I ask for your forgiveness and denounce those beliefs right now. I break every agreement that I have made with my sickness and disease. I denounce every symptom of my illness, and I ask to be set free by the power of your truth.

Please send forth your Holy Spirit to renew my mind and cleanse my thoughts. I refuse to bow down and serve the symptoms of my illness any longer. Please draw my attention away from myself, and help me focus on your enduring love.

O Divine Physician, you are the source and strength of my recovery. Show me how to proceed with your plan for my restoration. I surrender my healthcare into your loving hands. Please help me to discern every aspect of my treatment, medications and recovery process, so that my every thought and action conforms to your good and perfect will for my life. Amen.

Think, O God, of our friend who is ill, whom we now commend to Your compassionate regard.

Comfort him upon his sickbed, and ease his suffering. We beg for deliverance, and submit that no healing is too hard for the Lord, if it be His will.

We therefore pray that You bless our friend with Your loving care, renew his strength, and heal what ails him in Your loving name. Thank You, Lord. Amen.

Dear Lord, You are the Just judge, Holy and True. You are the Most High God. You give us life. You hold all power in your hands.

You are the Mighty one from God who carries the world, and is ruler over all the earth. You, Oh Most Blessed One, are the giver of life. In you are only good things. In you is mercy and love. In you is healing of the nations. In you is freedom of worry and freedom of pain.

Lord Almighty, You loved us so much. You were sent from your Father, sent to save us from destruction. We truly can never make it to Heaven without the help of Jesus the Son, who was sent to earth to help us.

You, Lord are full of mercy and grace, please forgive us for our faults. Lord Jesus, in you all healing is performed. You, Lord, are the miracle worker. In your Spirit, your gift of healing is alive. In you, Lord, we can put our trust that you can heal us, and protect us from the enemy, and death of our soul.

You, Lord, are miracle worker for the sick, and for the lost souls. You, Lord, forgive us and save us from condemnation. You cleanse us and make us born again new. You give us a clean heart full of peace. You, Lord, are the Light.

In You is all truth. Your way, Lord, is the way to Heavenly Hope. Your hands, Lord, created the universe. You, Lord, are the True giver of Life. Every child is a miracle of Life. Life rests in Your Hands.

Wrap us as a close-knit family, draw us near to you, Lord, and bind us with your Loving Hands. Let us be drawn closer to You. You are the Vine, dear Lord, and we are the branches. You carry all knowledge and all power. You, Lord, are our medicine. Your Words, Lord, are Truth and Life.

Help us put our trust in You. You, Lord, are the greatest physician. You heal, You protect, You care, You love, You are kind, You are patient, You are thoughtful, You are strength. You, Lord, are our Creator.

You know our thoughts, our sighing and our crying and every hair on our head. You are

Wonderful and make all good things for us.
Heal us, Lord, if it be Your will. Amen.

Lord, today I want to thank you for Your healing power at work in my life.

You have never left me alone.

You have been there with me through every problem.

You have healed me physically, emotionally and spiritually to health every time.

At times it has been a slow process, but I had to learn what You wanted me understand along the way. There are times that are still sensitive and difficult, but I know You are there if I let You in.

I know that there is power in the name of Jesus.

I know that when I call on You, Lord, that You can and will break every chain that keeps me from You. Lord, I know that while You were here You healed the lepers, restored sight to the blind, lifted the lame and raised the dead.

Thank You for continuing to show us miracles before our eyes of Your glory.

Lord, I thank you for hearing my prayers!

I thank You for hearing the prayers of prayer groups all over the world.

Thank You for listening and beating cancer when doctors have said it wasn't possible. Thank You for showing us over and over that with You nothing is impossible, not even the grave. Amen.

Almighty and merciful Father, by the power of your command, drive away from me all forms of sickness and disease. Restore strength to my body and joy to my spirit, so that in my renewed health, I may bless and serve you, now and forevermore. Amen.

Lord, You invite all who are burdened to come to You. Allow your healing hand to heal me. Touch my soul with Your compassion for others. Touch my heart with Your courage and infinite love for all. Touch my mind with Your wisdom, that my mouth may always proclaim Your praise. Teach me to reach out to You in my need, and help me to lead others to You by my example. Most loving Heart of Jesus, bring me health in body and spirit that I may serve You with all my strength. Touch gently this life which You have created, now and forever. Amen.

Lord, look upon me with eyes of mercy, may your healing hand rest upon me, may your life-giving powers flow into every cell of my body and into the depths of my soul, cleansing, purifying, restoring me to wholeness and strength for service in your Kingdom. Amen.

O God who are the only source of health and healing, the spirit of calm and the central peace of this universe, grant to me such a consciousness of your indwelling and surrounding presence that I may permit you to give me health and strength and peace, through Jesus Christ our Lord. Amen.

Healing Prayer of Isaiah 53

Precious Lord Jesus, I thank you for your enduring love. You came into the world to set me free from the power of darkness. You embraced a violent death on the cross to pay the penalty on my behalf. You suffered the scourging at the pillar, taking the sickness of humanity upon your own flesh, so that I could be healed.

I come before you now to place all my sin upon your cross and ask for your precious blood to wash me clean. I place the penalty for my sinfulness, all my sickness, diseases and infirmities upon your cross, and for the sake of your sorrowful passion, I ask to be set free. I accept your sacrifice and receive your gift of reconciliation. I confess your Lordship over every aspect of my life, heart, mind, body, soul and spirit.

Through the power of your cross, Lord Jesus, I now resist all forms of sin, sickness and disease. I say to all forms of sickness and disease caused by my own disobedience, that you are not God's good and perfect will for my life, and I enforce the power of the cross upon you right now.

By the shed blood of the Lord Jesus Christ of Nazareth, I command all forms of sickness and disease to leave my presence immediately. Jesus bore my infirmities. He was wounded for my transgressions. By his stripes I have been healed. No sickness, pain, death, fear or addiction shall ever be lord over me again. The penalty has been paid in full. I have been ransomed and redeemed, sanctified and set free. Amen.

Healing Prayer of Surrender

Dear Lord Jesus, it is my will to surrender to you everything that I am and everything that I'm striving to be. I open the deepest recesses of my heart and invite your Holy Spirit to dwell inside of me.

I offer you my life, heart, mind, body, soul, spirit, all my hopes, plans and dreams. I surrender to you my past, present and future problems, habits, character defects, attitudes, livelihood, resources, finances, medical coverage, occupation and all my relationships.

I give you my health, physical appearance, disabilities, family, marriage, children and friendships. I ask you to take Lordship over every aspect of my life. I surrender to you all my hurt, pain, worry, doubt, fear and anxiety, and I ask you to wash me clean.

I release everything into your compassionate care. Please speak to me clearly, Lord. Open my ears to hear your voice. Open my heart to commune with you more deeply. I want to feel your loving embrace. Open the doors that need to be opened and close the doors that need to be closed. Please set my feet upon the straight and narrow road that leads to everlasting life. Amen.

Inner Healing

Almighty and everlasting Lord, I come before you now in great need of your mercy. You are the doctor and physician of my soul. I humbly beseech thee to send forth your healing power into every area of my inner-woundedness. I surrender to you all areas of unforgiveness, especially those hurtful past events where anger and bitterness have been allowed to fester, causing harm to my physical health.

I ask for your grace to forgive every person in my past who has ever hurt me. I forgive my father and mother and ask to be set free from all forms of mental, emotional and psychological ailments. I forgive my brothers and sisters for their sibling rivalry, selfishness and divisiveness that have caused strife within our family. I forgive my friends, co-workers and neighbors for all their harmful actions and the unkind words they have spoken against me.

I forgive my spouse, children and all my extended family members, and I ask for your loving grace to heal all the circumstances where I failed to receive the love, affection, support and respect that I needed. I forgive all those who have violated my sexual purity, and I ask to be set free and washed clean by the power of your purifying love. I forgive myself for my past mistakes and failures, and I ask to be set free from all destructive consequences, guilt, shame and self-condemnation.

I forgive all those in positions of authority, especially those doctors, nurses, healthcare providers, insurance adjustors, paramedics, police officers, government officials, former employers and members of the clergy who have treated me unjustly. I forgive my greatest enemies and those who I have vowed that I would never forgive. I break those vows right now by the power of your name, Lord Jesus.

By an act of my free will, I choose to forgive everybody, including the person who hurt me the most. I release my desire to receive an apology, my need to be justified in my actions and my need for others to acknowledge the injustice. I surrender the entire debt of all injuries into your merciful hands, Lord Jesus. I denounce all forms of anger, bitterness and resentment, and I command every evil spirit that has entered my body through the lack of forgiveness to leave now and go straight to the feet of my Lord, Jesus Christ.

Through the power of your Holy Spirit, I ask you, Lord Jesus, to fill me with your love, peace, patience, kindness, generosity and self-control. May your healing hand rest upon me now as I bless all those who have hurt me. I desire to be kind and compassionate to everyone, forgiving them just as you have forgiven me. I ask for the healing power of your love to flow through every cell of my body and into the lives of those whom I have forgiven. Amen.

Life

Lord Jesus Christ, You know the pain of brokenness; You took our weaknesses upon Your shoulders and bore it to the wood of the cross. Hear our prayers for our brothers and sisters whose bodies fail them and whose minds are crippled by the ravages of disease. Implant a love for them deep within our hearts, that we, disfigured and disabled by our sin, may treasure and nurture the gifts of their lives. May we find You in their weakness, and console You in our care for them. For You are Lord, forever and ever. Amen.

O God, our Creator, all life is in your hands from conception until death. Help us to cherish our children and to reverence the awesome privilege of our share in creation. May all people live and die in dignity and love. Bless all those who defend the rights of the unborn, the handicapped and the aged. Enlighten and be merciful toward those who fail to love, and give them peace. Let freedom be tempered by responsibility, integrity and morality. Amen.

My Lighthouse of Hope

Most gracious and loving Father, I want to thank You for all the blessings You've given me, my family and friends and all those I hold dear.

Thank You, Lord, for giving me another day to see the beauty of your creations. You know the state of crisis that I am in now, Lord. I want to be of use again to You, Lord. In the time of my hospitalization, You, Lord, remain as my rock and my anchor.

You stand as my lighthouse giving me hope. I pray, Lord, that you will heal me soon. In Jesus' name. Amen.

Pain

Almighty Father, Thank you for your love, grace and mercy. I pray that my discomforts will turn to comforts, my pains to gains, my deprivation to more blessings, my losses to profits, my tear to smiles, my sorrows to pleasures, my illness to wellness, my debts to credits and my dreams to realities.

As the scripture said, "The Lord is near to the brokenhearted and saves the crushed in spirit." And "He heals the brokenhearted and binds up their wounds."

I trust in you, Lord, and in you alone to heal me with any form of skepticism towards blessing that you will be employed upon me. I trust, Lord, that this agony and suffering that is only in my head, will come to end and positivism will shine upon me as I read, hear, study and preach the truth in the Bible. Amen.

Recovery

Today I want to thank You, Lord, for my recovery.

Once I was broken, and You have brought me back and healed me.

Your loving kindness made me willing to give You all of me, the good and the bad.

You gave me strength over my addictions and impulses with forgiveness.

Thank You for the mercy that made me willing to face all of my defects of character.

Thank You for guiding me through it so that now I can be more useful to You and others around me. Lord, thank You for healing all of my physical, mental and emotional injuries.

Your way is so much easier, Your burden so much lighter.

When I rest in You, You do most of the work. When it is my time to be of service, I don't have to try that hard because it is a joy to serve.

Thank You for what I learned on the way to my recovery, that I may help those still stuck in sickness. Thank You for the message of the "Good Samaritan" to show me how to help others recover.

I pray You light a path in front of me that I may know Your hand is on my life. Amen.

Renewal of Mind, Body and Soul

Lord, I come before you today in need of your healing hand. In you all things are pos-

sible. Hold my heart within yours, and renew my mind, body, and soul.
I am lost, but I come to you with grace.
You gave us life, and you also give us the
gift of infinite joy. Give me the strength to
move forward on the path you've laid out
for me. Guide me towards better health, and
give me the wisdom to identify those you've
placed around me to help me get better.
In your name I pray, Amen.

Sickness

O Jesus, suffered and died for us; You understand suffering; Teach me to stand suffering
as You do; To bear it in union with You; To
offer it with You to atone for my sins, And
to bring Your grace to souls in need. Calm
fears; increase my trust. May I gladly accept
Your holy will and become more like You in
trial. If it be Your will, restore me to health
so that I may work for Your honor and glory and the salvation of all peoples. Amen.
Mary, help of the sick, pray for me.

Sickness or Trial

O good Jesus, I accept willingly this sickness [or trial] which it has pleased you to lay

upon me. I confide all my pains to your Sacred Heart, and beg you to unite them with your bitter sufferings, and thus perfect them by making them your own.

Since I cannot render you the praise due to you because of the multitude of my sorrows and afflictions, I ask you to praise God the Father for all I suffer, with the same tribute of praise you offered him when your agony on the Cross was at its height.

As you thanked him with all the powers of your soul for all the sufferings and injustice which he willed you should endure, so, I pray you, give him thanks for my trials also. Offer my sufferings, physical and spiritual, to him together with your most holy pains to his eternal honor and glory. Amen.

The Critically Ill

O Lord our God, You are the healer of all mankind. In Your merciful love you heal us of sin and the effects of sin in this life and the next. We pray to you, our Lord, this day to accelerate your plan of final healing and glory for our loved one. Call your beloved home to the fullness of happiness and glory with You for all eternity. Amen.

The Dying

Most Merciful Jesus, lover of souls, I pray to You, by the agony of Your most Sacred Heart, and by the sorrows of Your Immaculate Mother, to wash in our Most Precious Blood, the sinners of the world who are now in their agony and who will die today. Heart of Jesus, once in agony, have mercy on the dying. Amen.

The Dying

Lord Jesus Christ, as You stood by the bed of good Saint Joseph and gently led him home to heaven, so shepherd every soul about to die to a paradise of perfect peace. Let the tears we shed upon their passing stand witness to our love for them. Amen.

The Dying

Most merciful Jesus, lover of souls, I pray you by the agony of your most sacred heart, and by the sorrows of your Immaculate mother, to wash in your most Precious Blood the sinners of the world who are now in their agony, and who will die today.
Heart of Jesus, once in agony, have mercy on the dying.

Jesus, Mary and Joseph, I give you my heart and my soul. Assist me in my last agony, and grant that I may breathe forth my soul in peace with you. Amen.

The Sick

Dear Jesus, Divine Physician and Healer of the sick, we turn to you in this time of illness. O dearest comforter of the troubled, alleviate our worry and sorrow with your gentle love, and grant us the grace and strength to accept this burden. Dear God, we place our worries in your hands. We place our sick under your care and humbly ask that you restore your servant to health again. Above all, grant us the grace to acknowledge your will and know that whatever you do, you do for the love of us. Amen.

Watch, O Lord, with those who wake, or watch, or weep tonight, and give your angels charge over those who sleep.
Tend your sick ones, O Lord Christ.
Rest your weary ones.
Bless your dying ones.
Soothe your suffering ones.
Pity your afflicted ones.

Shield your joyous ones.
And for all your love's sake. Amen.
Saint Augustine

Dear Jesus, Divine Physician and Healer of the Sick, we turn to You in this time of illness. O dearest Comforter of the Troubled, alleviate our worry and sorrow with Your gentle love, and grant us the grace and strength to accept this burden. Dear God, we place our worries in Your hands. We place our sick under Your care and humbly ask that You restore Your servant to health again. Above all, grant us the grace to acknowledge Your holy will and know that whatsoever You do, You do for the love of us. Amen.

Father of goodness and love, hear our prayers for the sick members of our community and for all who are in need. Amid mental and physical suffering may they find consolation in your healing presence. Show your mercy as you close wounds, cure illness, make broken bodies whole and free downcast spirits. May these special people find lasting health and deliverance, and so join us in thanking you for all your gifts. We ask this through

the Lord Jesus who healed those who be-
lieved. Amen.

HOLY SPIRIT PRAYERS

Come Holy Spirit

Come Holy Spirit, fill the hearts of your
faithful and kindle in them the fire of your
love. Send forth your Spirit and they shall
be created. And You shall renew the face of
the earth.

O, God, who by the light of the Holy Spirit,
did instruct the hearts of the faithful, grant
that by the same Holy Spirit we may be
truly wise and ever enjoy His consolations,
Through Christ Our Lord, Amen.

Enlightenment

O Holy Spirit, divine Spirit of light and love,
I consecrate to Thee my understanding, my
heart and my will, my whole being for time
and for eternity. May my understanding be
always obedient to Thy heavenly inspirations and the teachings of the holy Catholic Church, of which Thou art the infallible
Guide; may my heart be ever inflamed with
love of God and of my neighbor; may my

will be ever conformed to the divine will, and may my whole life be a faithful following of the life and virtues of Our Lord and Savior Jesus Christ, to whom with the Father and Thee be honor and glory forever. Amen.

For the Help of the Holy Spirit

O God, send forth your Holy Spirit into my heart that I may perceive, into my mind that I may remember, and into my soul that I may meditate. Inspire me to speak with piety, holiness, tenderness and mercy. Teach, guide and direct my thoughts and senses from beginning to end. May your grace ever help and correct me, and may I be strengthened now with wisdom from on high, for the sake of your infinite mercy. Amen.
Saint Anthony of Padua

For the Gifts of the Holy Spirit

Holy Spirit, divine Consoler, I adore You as my true God, with God the Father and God the Son. I adore You and unite myself to the adoration You receive from the angels and saints.

I give You my heart and I offer my ardent thanksgiving for all the grace which You never cease to bestow on me.

O Giver of all supernatural gifts, who filled the soul of the Blessed Virgin Mary, Mother of God, with such immense favors, I beg You to visit me with Your grace and Your love and to grant me the gift of holy fear, so that it may act on me as a check to prevent me from falling back into my past sins, for which I beg pardon.

Grant me the gift of piety, so that I may serve You for the future with increased fervor, follow with more promptness Your holy inspirations, and observe your divine precepts with greater fidelity.

Grant me the gift of knowledge, so that I may know the things of God and, enlightened by Your holy teaching, may walk, without deviation, in the path of eternal salvation.

Grant me the gift of fortitude, so that I may overcome courageously all the assaults of the devil, and all the dangers of this world which threaten the salvation of my soul.

Grant me the gift of counsel, so that I may choose what is more conducive to my spiritual advancement and may discover the wiles and snares of the tempter.

Grant me the gift of understanding, so that I may apprehend the divine mysteries and by contemplation of heavenly things detach my thoughts and affections from the vain things of this miserable world.

Grant me the gift of wisdom, so that I may rightly direct all my actions, referring them to God as my last end; so that, having loved Him and served Him in this life, I may have the happiness of possessing Him eternally in the next. Amen.

Saint Alphonsus Liguori

For the Indwelling of the Spirit

Holy Spirit, powerful Consoler, sacred Bond of the Father and the Son, Hope of the afflicted, descend into my heart and establish in it your loving dominion. Enkindle in my tepid soul the fire of your Love so that I may be wholly subject to you. We believe that when you dwell in us, you also prepare a dwelling for the Father and the Son. Deign, therefore, to come to me, Consoler of abandoned souls, and Protector of the needy. Help the afflicted, strengthen the weak, and support the wavering. Come and purify me. Let no evil desire take possession of me. You

love the humble and resist the proud. Come to me, glory of the living, and hope of the dying. Lead me by your grace that I may always be pleasing to you. Amen.
Saint Augustine of Hippo

For the Seven Gifts of the Holy Spirit

O Lord Jesus Christ, Who, before ascending into heaven, didst promise to send the Holy Spirit to finish Thy work in the souls of Thy Apostles and Disciples, deign to grant the same Holy Spirit to me, that He may perfect in my soul the work of Thy grace and Thy love. Grant me the Spirit of Wisdom that I may despise the perishable things of this world and aspire only after the things that are eternal, the Spirit of Understanding to enlighten my mind with the light of Thy divine truth, the Spirit of Counsel that I may ever choose the surest way of pleasing God and gaining Heaven, the Spirit of Fortitude that I may bear my cross with Thee, and that I may overcome with courage all the obstacles that oppose my salvation, the Spirit of Knowledge that I may know God and know myself and grow perfect in the science of the Saints, the Spirit of Piety that I may find the service of God sweet and amiable, the Spirit of Fear that I may be filled with a loving reverence towards God, and may dread in any way to displease Him. Mark me, dear Lord, with the sign of Thy true disciples and animate me in all things with Thy Spirit. Amen.

Litany of the Holy Spirit

Lord, have mercy on us.

Christ, have mercy on us.

Lord, have mercy on us.

Father all powerful, have mercy on us.

Jesus, Eternal Son of the Father, Redeemer of the world, save us.

Spirit of the Father and the Son, boundless life of both, sanctify us.

Holy Trinity, hear us Holy Spirit, Who proceedest from the Father and the Son, enter our hearts.

Holy Spirit, Who art equal to the Father and the Son, enter our hearts.

Promise of God the Father, have mercy on us.

Ray of heavenly light, have mercy on us.

Author of all good, have mercy on us.

Source of heavenly water, have mercy on us.

Consuming fire, have mercy on us.

Ardent charity, have mercy on us.

Spiritual unction, have mercy on us.

Spirit of love and truth, have mercy on us

Spirit of wisdom and understanding, have mercy on us.

Spirit of counsel and fortitude, have mercy on us.

Spirit of knowledge and piety, have mercy on us.

Spirit of the fear of the Lord, have mercy on us.

Spirit of grace and prayer, have mercy on us.

Spirit of peace and meekness, have mercy on us.

Spirit of modesty and innocence, have mercy on us.

Holy Spirit, the Comforter, have mercy on us.

Holy Spirit, the Sanctifier, have mercy on us.

Holy Spirit, Who governest the Church, have mercy on us.

Gift of God, the Most High, have mercy on us.

Spirit Who fillest the universe, have mercy on us.

Spirit of the adoption of the children of God, have mercy on us.

Holy Spirit, inspire us with horror of sin.

Holy Spirit, come and renew the face of the earth.

Holy Spirit, shed Thy light in our souls.

Holy Spirit, engrave Thy law in our hearts.

Holy Spirit, inflame us with the flame of Thy love.

Holy Spirit, open to us the treasures of Thy graces.

Holy Spirit, teach us to pray well.

Holy Spirit, enlighten us with Thy heavenly inspirations.

Holy Spirit, lead us in the way of salvation

Holy Spirit, grant us the only necessary knowledge.

Holy Spirit, inspire in us the practice of good.

Holy Spirit, grant us the merits of all virtues.

Holy Spirit, make us persevere in justice.

Holy Spirit, be Thou our everlasting reward.

Lamb of God, Who takest away the sins of the world, Send us Thy Holy Spirit.

Lamb of God, Who takest away the sins of the world, pour down into our souls the gifts of the Holy Spirit.

Lamb of God, Who takest away the sins of the world, grant us the Spirit of wisdom and piety.

Come, Holy Spirit! Fill the hearts of Thy faithful, And enkindle in them the fire of Thy love. Let Us Pray.

Grant, 0 merciful Father, that Thy Divine Spirit may enlighten, inflame and purify us, that He may penetrate us with His heavenly dew and make us fruitful in good works, through Our Lord Jesus Christ, Thy Son, Who with Thee, in the unity of the same Spirit, liveth and reigneth forever and ever. Amen.

O Holy Spirit

Replace the tension within, with holy relaxation.

Replace the turbulence with a sacred calm.

Replace the anxiety with a quiet confidence.

Replace the fear with a strong faith.

Replace the darkness with a gentle light.

Replace the bitterness with the sweetness of Your Grace.

Replace the coldness within, with a gentle warmth.

O my loving Jesus, by the power of your Spirit make

of me, a 'praise of glory' to the Father. Amen.

The Holy Spirit

Breathe into me Holy Spirit, that all my thoughts may be holy. Move in me, Holy Spirit, that my work, too, may be holy. Attract my heart, Holy Spirit, that I may love only what is holy. Strengthen me, Holy Spirit, that I may defend all that is holy. Protect me, Holy Spirit, that I always may be holy. PRAYER TO THE HOLY SPIRIT: Spirit of wisdom and understanding, enlighten our minds to perceive the mysteries of the universe in relation to eternity. Spirit of right judgment and courage, guide us and make us firm in our baptismal decision to follow Jesus' way of love. Spirit of knowledge and reverence, help us to see the lasting value of justice and mercy in our everyday dealings with one another. May we respect life as we work to solve problems of family and nation, economy and ecology. Spirit of God, spark our faith, hope and love into new action each day. Fill our lives with wonder and awe in your presence which penetrates all creation. Amen.

Saint Augustine

Holy Spirit, Sweet guest of My Soul, Abide In Me and Grant That I May Ever abide in Thee. Amen.

Holy Spirit of light and love, you are the substantial love of the Father and the Son; hear my prayer. Bounteous bestower of most precious gifts, grant me a strong and living faith which makes me accept all revealed truths and shape my conduct in accord with them. Give me a most confident hope in all divine promises which prompts me to abandon myself unreservedly to you and your guidance. Infuse into me a love of perfect goodwill, and act according to God's least desires. Make me love not only my friends but my enemies as well, in imitation of Jesus Christ, who through you offered himself on the Cross for all people. Holy Spirit, animate, inspire, and guide me, and help me to be always a true follower of you. Amen.

Lord, today I want to thank You for gifting me with the Holy Spirit.
It is a gift that You have poured out for all, and I thank You for how much You have given me.
Lord, Your Word shows in the Bible that as soon as You gave us the Holy Spirit, wonderful things happened.

The Holy Spirit ignited a fire in believers and they were able to do great things.

They were able to perform miracles by healing people and speaking boldly in Your name.

Lord, without the Holy Spirit dwelling in me I would have never made it.

Your Holy Spirit has saved me and given me enormous strength that I wouldn't have had on my own.

Forgive me for where I have grieved the Holy Spirit with my decisions and actions.

Thank You that the Holy Spirit pulls me back to You with nudges and whispers and sometimes direct intervention.

Thank You, Jesus, that You said You must leave so we can have the Holy Spirit.

What a precious promise to strengthen my faith.

You said the Holy Spirit will counsel us, give us prophecy, and so many other gifts that I am overjoyed to have this in me.

Thank You for the wonderful Helper that is the Holy Spirit.

Lord, make me sensitive to Your urging, make me receptive to Your voice and bless me with the ability to talk to You more clearly and more often. Amen.

O Holy Spirit, You are the Third Person of the Blessed Trinity. You are the Spirit of truth, love and holiness, proceeding from the Father and the Son, and equal to Them in all things. I adore You and love You with all my heart. Teach me to know and to seek God, by whom and for whom I was created. Fill my heart with a holy fear and a great love for Him. Give me compunction and patience, and do not let me fall into sin.

Increase faith, hope and charity in me and bring forth in me all the virtues proper to my state of life. Help me to grow in the four cardinal virtues, Your seven gifts and Your twelve fruits.

Make me a faithful follower of Jesus, an obedient child of the Church and a help to my neighbor. Give me the grace to keep the commandments and to receive the sacraments worthily. Raise me to holiness in the state of life to which You have called me, and lead me through a happy death to everlasting life. Through Jesus Christ, our Lord. Grant me also, O Holy Spirit, Giver of all good gifts, the special favor for which I ask {name special petition}, if it be for Your honor and glory and for my well-being. Amen.

Spirit of wisdom and understanding, enlighten our minds to perceive the mysteries of the universe in relation to eternity. Spirit of right judgment and courage, guide us and make us firm in our baptismal decision to follow Jesus' way of love. Spirit of knowledge and reverence, help us to see the lasting value of justice and mercy in our everyday dealings with one another. May we respect life as we work to solve problems of family and nation, economy and ecology. Spirit of God, spark our faith, hope and love into new action each day. Fill our lives with wonder and awe in your presence which penetrates all creation. Amen.

We beseech you, O Lord, let the power of the Holy Spirit be always with us; let it mercifully purify our hearts, and safeguard us from all harm. Grant this through Christ our Lord, Amen.

May the Comforter, Who proceeds from You, enlighten our minds, we beseech you, O Lord, and guide us, as Your Son has promised, into all truth. We ask this through Christ, our Lord, Amen.

Veni Creator

Come, O Creator Spirit blest! And in our souls take up Thy rest; Come with Thy grace and heavenly aid, To fill the hearts which Thou hast made. Great Paraclete! To Thee we cry, O highest gift of God most high! O font of life! O fire of love! And sweet anointing from above.

Thou in Thy sevenfold gifts art known, The finger of God's hand we own; The promise of the Father, Thou! Who dost the tongue with power endow.

Kindle our senses from above, And make our hearts overflow with love; With patience firm and virtue high The weakness of our flesh supply.

Far from us drive the foe we dread, And grant us Thy true peace instead; So shall we not, with Thee for guide, Turn from the path of life aside.

Oh, may Thy grace on us bestow The Father and the Son to know, And Thee, through endless times confessed, Of both, the eternal Spirit blest.

All glory while the ages run Be to the Father and the Son Who rose from death; the same to Thee, O Holy Spirit, eternally. Amen.

PRAYERS FOR PEACE

Make Me an Instrument of Your Peace, Saint Francis Prayer

Lord, make me an instrument of Your peace. Where there is hatred, let me sow love; where there is injury, pardon; where there is doubt, faith; where there is despair, hope; where there is darkness, light; where there is sadness, joy.

O, Divine Master, grant that I may not so much seek to be consoled as to console; to be understood as to understand; to be loved as to love; For it is in giving that we receive; it is in pardoning that we are pardoned; it is in dying that we are born again to eternal life. Amen.

Peace

Lord, thank You that today I can have peace. Lord, I love how I can ask you for "peace that passes all understanding" and know You will hear me. Lord, I know that You are more powerful than anything here on earth. Thank You for giving me peace over my own emotions.

Lord, make me a channel for Your peace, that where there is hatred, I may bring love.

Lord, use the peace You put in me to be able to help wrongs turn into forgiveness.

Help me bring harmony where there was once discord.

Help me bring truth where there is doubt. Help me bring light where there is sadness.

Help me bring faith where there is despair.

Lord, help me to seek rather to comfort than be comforted, to understand, rather than be understood and to love, rather than be loved.

Lord, thank You for teaching me that it is by self-forgetting that I find, that it is by forgiving that I am forgiven and that it is by dying that I awaken to eternal life. Amen.

O Lord Jesus Christ, who said to Your Apostles: "Peace I leave with you, My peace I give to you," regard not my sins but the faith of Your Church, and deign to give her peace and unity according to Your Will: Who live and reign, God, world without end. Amen.

O Lord Jesus Christ, Who said to Your Apostles, "Peace I leave with you, My peace I give to you," regard not my sins but the faith of Your Church, and deign to give her peace and unity according to Your Will: Who live and reign, God, world without end. Amen.

CATHOLIC PRAYERS

Anima Christi

Soul of Christ, sanctify me.
Body of Christ, save me.
Blood of Christ, inebriate me.
Water from the side of Christ, wash me.
Passion of Christ, strengthen me.
O Good Jesus, hear me.
Within Thy wounds hide me.
Suffer me not to be separated from thee.
From the malignant enemy defend me.
In the hour of my death call me.
And bid me come unto Thee,
That with all Thy saints,
I may praise thee.
Forever and ever. Amen.

Apostles Creed

I believe in God, the Father Almighty,
Creator of heaven and earth;
And in Jesus Christ, His only Son, our Lord;
Who was conceived by the Holy Spirit, Born
of the Virgin Mary, Suffered under Pontius
Pilate, Was crucified, died, and was buried.
He descended into hell;
The third day he rose again from the dead;

He ascended into Heaven,
And is seated at the right hand of God,
the Father Almighty; From thence he shall
come to judge the living and the dead.
I believe in the Holy Spirit, The Holy Catholic Church, The Communion of Saints, The
forgiveness of sins, The resurrection of the
body, And life everlasting. Amen.

Beatitudes

Blessed are the poor in spirit, for theirs is
the kingdom of Heaven.

Blessed are the meek, for they shall possess
the earth.

Blessed are they who hunger and thirst for
justice, for they shall be satisfied.

Blessed are the merciful, for they shall obtain mercy.

Blessed are the clean of heart, for they shall
see God.

Blessed are the peacemakers, for they shall
be called children of God.

Blessed are they who suffer persecution
for justice sake, for theirs is the kingdom
of heaven.

Blessed are you who men reproach you,
and persecute you, and speaking falsely, say

all manner of evil against you, for my sake. Amen.

Dedication to Jesus

Lord Jesus Christ, take all my freedom, my memory, my understanding, and my will. All that I have and cherish you have given me. I surrender it all to be guided by your will. Your love and your grace are wealth enough for me. Give me these, Lord Jesus, and ask for nothing more. Amen.

Divine Praises

Blessed be God.
Blessed be His Holy Name.
Blessed be Jesus Christ, true God and true Man.
Blessed be the Name of Jesus.
Blessed be His Most Sacred Heart.
Blessed be His Most Precious Blood.
Blessed be Jesus in the Most Holy Sacrament of the Altar.
Blessed be the Holy Spirit, the Paraclete.
Blessed be the Great Mother of God, Mary Most holy.
Blessed her Holy and Immaculate Conception.

Blessed be her glorious Assumption.

Blessed be the name of Mary, Virgin and Mother.

Blessed be Saint Joseph, her most chaste spouse.

Blessed be God in His Angels and in His Saints.

May the heart of Jesus, in the Most Blessed Sacrament, be praised, adored, and loved with grateful affection, at every moment, in all the tabernacles of the world, even to the end of time. Amen.

Evening Prayer

Watch, O Lord, with those who wake, or watch, or weep tonight, and give Your Angels and Saints charge over those who sleep. Tend Your sick ones, O Lord Jesus Christ. Rest Your ones, Bless Your dying ones, Soothe Your suffering ones, Pity Your afflicted ones, Shield Your joyous ones, And all for Your love's sake. Amen.

I adore You, my God, and I love You with all my heart. I thank you for having created me, for having made me a Christian, and for having preserved me this day. Pardon me for the evil I have done today. If I have done anything good, be pleased to accept it. Protect me while I take my rest and deliver me from all dangers. May your grace be always with me. Amen.

Oh Lord, we pray you to visit this home and drive from it all snares of the enemy. Let Your holy angels dwell in it to preserve us in peace; and let Your blessing be always upon us. Through Christ our Lord. Amen.

Protect us, Lord, as we stay awake; watch over us as we sleep, that awake, we may keep watch with Christ, and asleep, rest in his peace. Amen

Gloria

Glory to God in the highest, and on earth peace to people of good will. We praise you, we bless you, we adore you, we glorify you, we give you thanks for your great glory, Lord God, heavenly King, O God, almighty Father. Lord Jesus Christ, Only Begotten Son, Lord God, Lamb of God, Son of the Father, you take away the sins of the world, have mercy on us; you take away the sins of the world, receive our prayer; you are seated at the right hand of the Father, have mercy on us. For you alone are the Holy One, you alone are the Lord, you alone are the Most High, Jesus Christ, with the Holy Spirit, in the glory of God the Father. Amen.

Glory Be

Glory be to the Father,
and to the Son,
and to the Holy Spirit.
As it was in the beginning,
is now, and ever shall be,
world without end. Amen.

God's blessing

O Lord, into Your hands and into the hands of Your holy angels, this day I entrust my soul, my relatives, my benefactors, my friends and enemies, and all Your Catholic people. O Lord, by the merits and prayers of the Blessed Virgin Mary and of all Your saints, keep us today from all evil and unruly desires, from all sins and temptations of the devil, from a sudden and unprovoked death, and from the pains of hell. Enlighten my heart with the grace of Your Holy Spirit. Grant that I may ever be obedient to Your commandments. Let me never be separated from You, O God, who live and reign with

God the Father and the same Holy Spirit forever. Amen.

Grace Before Meals

Bless us, O Lord, and these Your gifts which we are about to receive from Your bounty. Through Christ our Lord. Amen.

Grace After Meals

We give you thanks, Almighty God, for all Your benefits, who live and reign, world without end. Amen. May the souls of the faithful departed, through the mercy of God, rest in peace. Amen.

Guardian Angel

Angel of God's light, whom God sends as a companion for me on earth, protect me from the snares of the devil, and help me to walk always as a child of God, my Creator. Angel of God's truth, whose perfect knowledge serves what is true, protect me from deceits and temptations. Help me to know the truth, and always to live the truth. Angel of God's love, who praises Jesus Christ, the only Son of God, who sacrificed His life for love of us, sustain me as I learn the ways of divine love, of sacrificial generosity, of meekness and lowliness of heart. Thank You, my heavenly friend, for your watchful care. At the moment of my death, bring me to heaven, where the one true God, Who is light, Truth and Love, lives and reigns forever and ever. Amen.

Morning Offering

O Jesus, through the Immaculate Heart of Mary, I offer You my prayers, works, joys and sufferings of this day for all the intentions of Your Sacred Heart, in union with the Holy Sacrifice of the Mass throughout the world, in reparation for my sins, for the intentions of all my relatives and friends, and in particular for the intentions of the Holy Father. Amen.

Lord God Almighty, You have brought us safely to the beginning of this day. Defend us in it by Your mighty power, that this day we may not fall into sin, but that all our words may be spoken and all our thoughts and actions directed in such a manner as always to be pleasing in Your sight. Through Christ our Lord. Amen.

Lord, we beg of you, go before us with Your gracious inspiration in all our doings, and help us with your continual assistance, that our every prayer and work may begin from You and be duly ended by You. Through Christ our Lord. Amen.

Nicene Creed

We believe in one God, the Father, the Almighty,
of all that is, seen and unseen.
We believe in one Lord, Jesus Christ, the only Son of God,
eternally begotten of the Father, God from God, Light from Light,
true God from true God, begotten, not made, of one Being with the Father.
Through him all things were made.
For us and for our salvation he came down from heaven:
by the power of the Holy Spirit he became incarnate from the Virgin Mary, and was made man.
For our sake he was crucified under Pontius Pilate; he suffered death and was buried.

On the third day he rose again in accordance with the Scriptures;

he ascended into heaven and is seated at the right hand of the Father. He will come again in glory to judge the living and the dead, and his kingdom will have no end.

We believe in the Holy Spirit, the Lord, the giver of life, who proceeds from the Father and the Son. With the Father and the Son he is worshipped and glorified.

He has spoken through the Prophets. We believe in one holy catholic and apostolic Church.

We acknowledge one baptism for the forgiveness of sins.

We look for the resurrection of the dead, and the life of the world to come. Amen.

Novena to the Divine Child Jesus

Divine Child Jesus, we believe in You; We adore You; and we love You; have mercy on us, sinners. We've come to this Temple in response to your love. We've come in response to your mercy and grace. We are here because You invited us to come before You and to pour out the cares of our hearts to You since You deeply care for each of us. We remember Your words to the disciples: Ask and you shall receive. Seek and you shall find. Knock and the door shall be opened. Trusting in your infinite goodness and trusting that You always keep your promise, we now ask this intention which we pray in the silence of our hearts...silently mention the request... Thank you, Divine Child Jesus, for listening attentively to our prayers all the time. We hope that You will ask this before Our Heavenly Father. And, if what we ask for may not be good for our salvation and sanctification, we trust that you will grant us instead what we truly need, so that one day we may be with You for all eternity enjoying that ultimate happiness of Heaven. Divine Child Jesus, bless and protect us. Divine Child Jesus, bless and lead us. Divine Child Jesus, bless and provide for us. All this we ask through the intercession of your Holy Mother, Mary, and in Your powerful and Most Holy Name, Jesus. Amen.

Nuptial Blessing, Shorter
Be appeased, O Lord, by our humble prayers, and in Your kindness, assist this institution of marriage which You have ordained for the

propagation of the human race, so that this union made here, joined by Your authority, may be preserved by Your help. Through the same our Lord Jesus Christ, Your Son, Who lives and reigns with You in the unity of the Holy Spirit, God, world without end. Amen.

Nuptial Blessing, Longer

O God, by Your mighty power You made all things out of nothing. First, You set the beginnings of the universe in order. Then, You made man in Your image, and appointed woman to be his inseparable helpmate. Thus You made woman's body from the flesh of man, thereby teaching that what You have been pleased to institute from one principle might never lawfully be put asunder. O God, You have sanctified marriage by a mystery so excellent that in the marriage union You foreshadowed the union of Christ and the Church. O God, You join woman to man, and You endow that fellowship with a blessing which was not taken away in punishment for original sin nor by the sentence of the flood. Look, in Your mercy, upon this Your handmaid, about to be joined in wedlock, who entreats You to protect and strengthen her. Let the yoke of marriage to her be one of love and peace. Faithful and chaste, let her marry in Christ. Let her ever follow the model of holy women: let her be dear to her husband like Rachel; wise like Rebecca; long-lived and faithful like Sara. Let the author of sin work none of his evil deeds within her; let her ever keep the Faith and the commandments. Let her be true to one wedlock and shun all sinful embraces; let her strengthen weakness by stern discipline. Let her be grave in demeanor, honorable for her modesty, learned in heavenly doctrine, fruitful in children. Let her life be good and innocent. Let her come finally to the rest of the blessed in the kingdom of heaven. May they both see their children's children to the third and fourth generation, thus attaining the old age which they desire. Through the same our Lord Jesus Christ, Your Son, Who lives and reigns with You in the unity of the Holy Spirit, God, world without end. Amen.

Our Father

Our Father, Who art in heaven,
Hallowed be Thy Name.
Thy Kingdom come.

Thy Will be done, on earth as it is in Heaven. Give us this day our daily bread.
And forgive us our trespasses,
as we forgive those who trespass against us.
And lead us not into temptation,
but deliver us from evil. Amen.

Universal Prayer
(attributed to Pope Clement XI)
Lord, I believe in you: increase my faith.
I trust in you: strengthen my trust.
I love you: let me love you more and more.
I am sorry for my sins: deepen my sorrow.
I worship you as my first beginning,
I long for you as my last end,
I praise you as my constant helper,
And call on you as my loving protector.
Guide me by your wisdom,
Correct me with your justice,
Comfort me with your mercy,
Protect me with your power.
I offer you, Lord, my thoughts: to be fixed on you;
My words: to have you for their theme;
My actions: to reflect my love for you;
My sufferings: to be endured for your greater glory.

I want to do what you ask of me:
In the way you ask,
For as long as you ask,
Because you ask it.
Lord, enlighten my understanding,
Strengthen my will,
Purify my heart,
and make me holy.
Help me to repent of my past sins.
And to resist temptation in the future.
Help me to rise above my human weaknesses
And to grow stronger as a Christian.
Let me love you, my Lord and my God,
And see myself as I really am:
A pilgrim in this world,
A Christian called to respect and love
All whose lives I touch,
Those under my authority,
My friends and my enemies.
Help me to conquer anger with gentleness,
Greed by generosity,
Apathy by fervor.
Help me to forget myself
And reach out toward others.
Make me prudent in planning,
Courageous in taking risks.
Make me patient in suffering, unassuming
in prosperity.

Keep me, Lord, attentive at prayer,
Temperate in food and drink,
Diligent in my work,
Firm in my good intentions.
Let my conscience be clear,
My conduct without fault,
My speech blameless,
My life well-ordered.
Put me on guard against my human weaknesses.
Let me cherish your love for me,
Keep your law,
And come at last to your salvation.
Teach me to realize that this world is passing,
That my true future is the happiness of heaven,
That life on earth is short,
And the life to come eternal.
Help me to prepare for death
With a proper fear of judgment,
But a greater trust in your goodness.
Lead me safely through death.
To the endless joy of heaven.
Grant this through Christ our Lord. Amen.

PRAYERS FOR THE CHURCH

Priests

Heavenly Father, bless and protect priests and fill them with the joy and courage of their vocation as personal ministers of Christ in preaching Your word, forming communities in Your name and nourishing us with the Sacraments. We ask this through Christ our Lord. Amen.

O Jesus, I pray for your faithful and fervent priests; for Your unfaithful and tired priests; for Your priests laboring at home or abroad in distant mission fields; for Your tempted priests; for Your lonely priests; for Your young priests; for Your dying priests; for the souls of Your priests in purgatory.

But above all, I recommend to You the priests dearest to me; the priest who baptized me; the priests who absolved me from my sins; the priests at whose Masses I assisted and who gave me Your Body and Blood in Holy Communion; the priests who taught and instructed me; all the priests to whom I am indebted in any other way. O Jesus, keep them all close to Your heart, and bless them abundantly in time and eternity. Amen.

The Church

Heavenly Father, look upon our community of faith which is the Church of Your Son, Jesus Christ. Help us to witness to His love by loving all our fellow creatures without exception. Under the leadership of the Holy Father and the Bishops keep us faithful to Christ's mission of calling all men and women to Your service so that there may be "one fold and one shepherd." We ask this through Christ our Lord. Amen.

The Laity

Heavenly Father, You have called us all to holiness, which means sharing in Your divine life. Fill us with a sense of our true dignity as those called to be Your daughters and sons in the world and Your ambassadors of justice, love and peace. Give us the desire to be worthy of this great calling and the courage to live up to it. We ask this through Christ our Lord. Amen.

The Pope

Heavenly Father, be pleased to bless and protect our Holy Father, our Pope, whom You have chosen as the successor of Saint Peter to be chief minister of unity and charity in the Church. Keep him safe in holiness of life and in wise fulfillment of his responsibilities. We ask this through Christ our Lord. Amen.

Vocations

Lord of the harvest, your Word finds a home in our hearts, calls us into community and invites to generous service of the human family. Bless with courage and spirit your priestly people called to full participation in the one Body of Christ. May many choose to respond in public service to your call offered in Jesus' name. Amen.

O Father, inspire among Christians many holy vocations to the priesthood that keep alive the faith and preserve the grateful memory of your son Jesus through preaching his Word and administering the Sacraments with which you ceaselessly renew your faithful.

Call forth ministers of your mercy who, through the sacrament of Reconciliation, may spread the joy of your forgiveness.

O Father, make the Church welcome joyously the many inspirations of the Spirit of your Son and, docile to His teachings, nurture vocations to the priestly ministry and to the consecrated life.

Support the bishops, priests and deacons, the consecrated persons and all the baptized in Christ, so that they may faithfully fulfill their mission at the service of the Gospel.

We ask for this through Christ our Lord. Amen.

Mary, Queen of the Apostles, pray for us!
Pope Benedict XVI

Vocations

Lord, let me know clearly the work that You are calling me to do in life. And grant me every grace I need to answer Your call with courage and love and lasting dedication to Your will. Amen.

O God, you sent your Son, Jesus, to bring eternal life to those who believe. I join him in praying for laborers for your harvest. May your Holy Spirit inspire men and women to continue his mission through your priesthood, diaconate, religious life and lay ministry. May this same Spirit make known your will for my life. Amen

PRAYERS FOR MARY'S INTERCESSION

Angelus V.

The Angel of the Lord declared unto Mary,
R. And she conceived of the Holy Spirit.
Hail Mary, etc.
V. Behold the handmaid of the Lord.
R. Be it done to me according to Your Word.
Hail Mary, etc.
V. And the Word was made flesh,
R. And dwelt among us. Hail Mary, etc.
Let us Pray:
Pour forth, we beseech You, O Lord, Your Grace into our hearts; that as we have known the incarnation of Christ Your Son by the message of an angel, so by His passion and cross we may be brought to the glory of His resurrection.
Through the same Christ, our Lord. Amen.

Hail Mary

Hail Mary, Full of Grace,
The Lord is with thee.
Blessed art thou among women,
and blessed is the fruit of thy womb, Jesus.
Holy Mary, Mother of God,
pray for us sinners now,
and at the hour of death. Amen.

Litany of Mary

Lord, have mercy.

Christ, have mercy.

Lord, have mercy.

God our Father In Heaven, have mercy on us.

God the Son, Redeemer of the world, have mercy on us.

God the Holy Spirit, have mercy on us.

Holy Trinity, one God, have mercy on us.

Holy Mary, pray for us.

Holy Mother of God, pray for us.

Most honored of virgins, pray for us.

Mother of Christ, pray for us.

Mother of the Church, pray for us.

Mother of divine grace, pray for us.

Mother most pure, pray for us.

Mother of chaste love, pray for us.

Mother and virgin, pray for us.

Sinless Mother, pray for us.

Dearest of Mothers, pray for us.

Model of motherhood, pray for us.

Mother of good counsel, pray for us.

Mother of our Creator, pray for us.

Mother of our Savior, pray for us.

Virgin most wise, pray for us.

Virgin rightly praised, pray for us.

Virgin rightly renowned, pray for us.

Virgin most powerful, pray for us.
Virgin gentle in mercy, pray for us.
Faithful Virgin, pray for us.
Mirror of justice, pray for us.
Throne of wisdom, pray for us.
Cause of our joy, pray for us.
Shrine of the Spirit, pray for us.
Glory of Israel, pray for us.
Vessel of selfless devotion, pray for us.
Mystical Rose, pray for us.
Tower of David, pray for us.
Tower of ivory, pray for us.
House of gold, pray for us.
Ark of the covenant, pray for us.
Gate of heaven, pray for us.
Morning star, pray for us.
Health of the sick, pray for us.
Refuge of sinners, pray for us.
Comfort of the troubled, pray for us.
Help of Christians, pray for us.
Queen of angels, pray for us.
Queen of patriarchs and prophets, pray for us.
Queen of apostles and martyrs, pray for us.
Queen of confessors and virgins, pray for us.
Queen of all saints, pray for us.
Queen conceived without sin, pray for us.
Queen assumed in to heaven, pray for us

Queen of the rosary, pray for us.
Queen of families, pray for us.
Queen of peace, pray for us.
Blessed be the name of the Virgin Mary now and forever. Amen.

Magnificat - The Prayer Of Mary

My soul proclaims the greatness of the Lord, my spirit rejoices in God my Saviour for he has looked with favor on his lowly servant. From this day all generations will call me blessed: the Almighty has done great things for me, and holy is his Name. He has mercy on those who fear him in every generation. He has shown the strength of his arm, he has scattered the proud in their conceit. He has cast down the mighty from their thrones, and has lifted up the lowly. He has filled the hungry with good things, and the rich he has sent away empty. He has come to the help of his servant Israel for he remembered his promise of mercy, the promise he made to our fathers, to Abraham and his children forever. Amen. (Luke 1:46-55)

Mary, Mother of Grace

Mary, mother of grace, Mother of mercy, shield me from the enemy and receive me at the hour of my death. Amen.

Memorare

Remember, O most gracious Virgin Mary, that never was it known that anyone who fled to thy protection, implored thy help, or sought thine intercession was left unaided. Inspired by this confidence, I fly unto thee, O Virgin of virgins, my mother; to thee do I come, before thee I stand, sinful and sorrowful. O Mother of the Word Incarnate, despise not my petitions, but in thy mercy hear and answer me. Amen.

Prayer To Our Lady, Help Of Christians

Most Holy Virgin Mary, Help of Christian, how sweet it is to come to your feet imploring your perpetual help.
If earthly mothers cease not to remember their children,
how can you, the most loving of all mothers forget me?
Grant then to me, I implore you,
your perpetual help in all my necessities,

in every sorrow, and especially in all my temptations.

I ask for your unceasing help for all who are now suffering.

Help the weak, cure the sick, convert sinners. Grant through your intercessions many vocations to the religious life.

Obtain for us, O Mary, Help of Christians, that having invoked you on earth we may love and eternally thank you in heaven. Amen.

Saint John Bosco

ROSARY

You start the Rosary by saying the Apostles' Creed **on the cross, followed by one** Our Father, three Hail Marys and one Glory Be. Then you say the five decades of the Rosary. Each decade consists of one Our Father, followed by ten Hail Marys (which are said on each of ten beads grouped together), one Glory Be, and then the Fatima Prayer (below).

The Fatima Prayer

Oh my Jesus, forgive us our sins save us from the fires of hell, lead all souls to heaven especially those most in need of thy mercy.

During each decade you meditate on the following events in the lives of Jesus and Mary:

The Five Joyful Mysteries (said on Mondays and Saturdays)
1. The Annunciation
2. The Visitation
3. The Nativity
4. The Presentation
5. The Finding of the Child Jesus in the Temple

The Five Luminous Mysteries (Said on Thursdays)
1. The Baptism of Jesus
2. The Wedding at Cana
3. The Proclamation of the Kingdom of God
4. The Transfiguration
5. The Institution of the Eucharist

The Five Sorrowful Mysteries (said on Tuesdays and Fridays)

1. The Agony in the Garden
2. The Scourging at the Pillar
3. The Crowning with Thorns
4. The Carrying of the Cross
5. The Crucifixion

The Five Glorious Mysteries (said on Wednesdays and Sundays)

1. The Resurrection
2. The Ascension
3. The Descent of the Holy Spirit
4. The Assumption
5. The Coronation

Conclude with the Hail Holy Queen

Salve Regina - Hail Holy Queen

Hail, Holy Queen, Mother of Mercy. Hail our life, our sweetness and our hope! To you do we cry, poor banished children of Eve! To do we send up our sighs; mourning and weeping in this vale of tears! Turn then, most gracious, Advocate, Your eyes of mercy toward us; and after this our exile, show unto us the blessed of Your womb, Jesus! O Clement, O loving, O sweet Virgin Mary! Amen.

PRAYERS OF THE SAINTS

Saint Dominic

May God the Father who made us bless us. May God the Son send his healing among us. May God the Holy Spirit move within us and give us eyes to see with, ears to hear with, and hands that your work might be done.

May we walk and preach the word of God to all.

May the angel of peace watch over us and lead us at last by God's grace to the Kingdom. Amen.

Saint Francis de Sales

Patron Saint of writers and journalists

Be at Peace

Do not look forward in fear to the changes of life; rather look to them with full hope as they arise.

God, whose very own you are, will deliver you from out of them.

He has kept you hitherto, and He will lead you safely through all things; and when you cannot stand it, God will bury you in his arms.

Do not fear what may happen tomorrow; the same everlasting Father who cares for you today will take care of you then and every day.

He will either shield you from suffering, or will give you unfailing strength to bear it.

Be at peace, and put aside all anxious thoughts and imagination. Amen.

Confidence in God

It is good to mistrust ourselves, but how would that advantage us were we not to throw all our confidence on God, and to wait on His mercy? If you feel no such confidence, cease not on that account from making these acts and from saying to Our Lord: "Yet, O Lord, though I have no feeling of confidence in You, nevertheless, I know that You are my God, that I am all Yours, and that I have no hope but in Your goodness; so, I abandon myself entirely into Your Hands." It is always in our power to make these acts; although we have difficulty in performing them, still there is no impossibility. Thus we testify faithfulness to our Lord. Amen.

Direction of Intention

My God, I give you this day. I offer you, now, all of the good that I shall do and I promise to accept, for love of you, all of the difficulty that I shall meet. Help me to conduct myself during this day in a manner pleasing to you. Amen.

Your Cross

The everlasting God has in His wisdom foreseen from eternity the cross that He now presents to you as a gift from His inmost heart. This cross He now sends you He has considered with His all-knowing eyes, understood with His divine mind, tested with His wise justice, warmed with loving arms and weighed with His own hands to see that it be not one inch too large and not one ounce too heavy for you. He has blessed it with His Holy Name, anointed it with His consolation, taken one last glance at you and your courage, and then sent it to you from heaven, a special greeting from God to you, an alms of the all-merciful love of God. Amen.

Saint Francis of Assisi

Lord, make me a channel of thy peace, that where there is hatred, I may bring love; that where there is wrong, I may bring the spirit of forgiveness; that where there is discord, I may bring harmony; that where there is error, I may bring truth; that where there is doubt, I may bring faith; that where there is despair, I may bring hope; that where there are shadows, I may bring light; that where there is sadness, I may bring joy.

Lord, grant that I may seek rather to comfort than to be comforted; to understand, than to be understood; to love, than to be loved.

For it is by self-forgetting that one finds.
It is by forgiving that one is forgiven.

It is by dying that one awakens to Eternal Life. Amen.

Song of Saint Francis

Lord of my origin
Draw me closer to you
Lord of my existence
Direct all my ways
Lord of my calling
Give me strength to go on
Lord of my faith
Preserve me from doubt
Lord of my hope
Keep me from despair
Lord of my love
Let me never grow cold
Lord of my past
May I never forget you
Lord of my present
Be near me always
Lord of my future
Keep me faithful to the end
Lord of my life
Let me live in your presence
Lord of my death
Receive me at last
Lord of my eternity

Bless me forever. Amen.

Saint Ignatius of Loyola - Suscipe – means to receive

Take, O Lord, and receive my entire liberty, my memory, my understanding and my whole will. All that I am and all that I possess, Thou hast given me: I surrender it all to Thee to be disposed of according to Thy will. Give me only Thy love and Thy grace; with these I will be rich enough and will desire nothing more. Amen.

Saint Ignatius of Loyola - Prayer for Generosity

Teach me true generosity.
Teach me to serve you as you deserve.
To give without counting the cost,
To fight heedless of wounds,
To labor without seeking rest,
To sacrifice myself without thought of any reward
Save the knowledge that I have done your will. Amen.

Prayer Against Depression

O Christ Jesus

When all is darkness
And we feel our weakness and helplessness,
Give us the sense of Your Presence,
Your Love and Your Strength.
Help us to have perfect trust
In Your protecting love
And strengthening power,
So that nothing may frighten or worry us,
For, living close to You,
We shall see Your Hand,
Your Purpose, Your Will through all things.
Amen.

John Henry
Cardinal Newman

Dear Jesus, help me to spread your fragrance
everywhere I go;
Flood my soul with your spirit and life;
Penetrate and possess my whole being
so completely
That all my life may be only a radiance
of yours;
Shine through me and be so in me
That everyone with whom I come into contact
May feel your presence within me.
Let them look up and see no longer me—
but only Jesus. Amen.

Saint Michael

Saint Michael, the Archangel, defend us in battle; be our defense against the wickedness and snares of the devil. May God rebuke him, we humbly pray; and do you, O Prince of the heavenly Host, by the power of God, thrust into hell Satan and the other evil spirits who prowl about the world for the ruin of souls. Amen.

Saint Michael the Archangel

Saint Michael the Archangel,
defend us in battle.
Be our defense against the wickedness and snares of the Devil.
May God rebuke him, we humbly pray,
and do thou, O Prince of the heavenly hosts,
by the power of God, thrust into hell Satan,
and all the evil spirits, who prowl about the world
seeking the ruin of souls. Amen.

Saint Patrick

Christ be with me,
Christ before me,
Christ behind me,
Christ in me,
Christ beneath me,
Christ above me,
Christ on my right,
Christ on my left,
Christ where I lie,
Christ where I arise,
Christ in the heart of everyone who thinks
of me,
Christ in the mouth of everyone who speaks
of me,
Christ in the eye that sees me,
Christ in the ear that hears me,
In the name of Jesus. Amen.

Saint Pio Prayer of Trust & Confidence

O Lord, we ask for a boundless confidence
and trust in Your divine mercy, and the
courage to accept the crosses and sufferings
which bring immense goodness to our souls
and that of Your Church.

Help us to love You with a pure and contrite
heart, and to humble ourselves beneath Your

cross, as we climb the mountain of holiness, carrying our cross that leads to heavenly glory. May we receive You with great faith and love in Holy Communion, and allow You to act in us, as You desire, for Your greater glory.

O Jesus, most adorable heart and eternal fountain of Divine Love, may our prayer find favor before the Divine Majesty of Your Heavenly Father. Amen.

Saint Teresa of Avila

Let nothing disturb you,
Let nothing frighten you,
All things are passing away:
God never changes.
Patience obtains all things.
Whoever has God lacks nothing;
God alone suffices. Amen.

Saint Therese of Lisieux
A morning prayer

O my God! I offer Thee all my actions of this day for the intentions and for the glory of the Sacred Heart of Jesus. I desire to sanctify every beat of my heart, my every thought, my simplest works, by uniting them to its infinite merits; and I wish to make reparation for my sins by casting them into the furnace of Its Merciful Love.

O my God! I ask of Thee for myself and for those whom I hold dear, the grace to fulfill perfectly Thy Holy Will, to accept for love of Thee the joys and sorrows of this passing life, so that we may one day be united together in heaven for all Eternity. Amen.
Saint Thomas Aquinas

Saint Thomas Aquinas

Lord, Father all-powerful and ever-living God, I thank You, for

even though I am a sinner, your unprofitable servant, not

because of my worth but in the kindness of your mercy,

You have fed me with the Precious Body & Blood of Your Son,

our Lord Jesus Christ.

I pray that this Holy Communion may not bring me

condemnation and punishment but forgiveness and salvation.

May it be a helmet of faith and a shield of good will.

May it purify me from evil ways and put an end to my evil passions.

May it bring me charity and patience, humility and obedience,

and growth in the power to do good.

May it be my strong defense against all my enemies, visible and invisible, and the perfect calming of all my evil impulses, bodily and spiritual.

May it unite me more closely to you, the One true God, and lead me

safely through death to everlasting happiness with You.

And I pray that You will lead me, a sinner, to the banquet where you,

with Your Son and holy Spirit, are true and perfect light, total fulfillment, everlasting joy, gladness without end, and perfect happiness to your saints. grant this through Christ our Lord, Amen.

MASS PRAYERS

Prayers before Holy Communion

Prayer for Peace before Holy Communion

O Lord Jesus Christ, who said to Your Apostles: "Peace I leave with you, My peace I give to you," regard not my sins but the faith of Your Church, and deign to give her peace and unity according to Your Will: Who live and reign, God, world without end. Amen.

Your Sacred Table

Divine Savior, we come to Your sacred table to nourish ourselves, not with bread but with Yourself, true Bread of eternal life. Help us daily to make a good and perfect meal of this divine food. Let us be continually refreshed by the perfume of Your kindness and goodness. May the Holy Spirit fill us with His Love. Meanwhile, let us prepare a place for this holy food by emptying our hearts. Amen.

Saint Francis de Sales

Prayer for Holy Communion

O my God, how displeasing my sins are to you.

Forgive me, cleanse me.

Help me to sing the perfect Kyrie Eleison. Come into my soul, and find it pleasing. Repose in my heart. Let Thy entirety, sweet Jesus, of Thee in the Eucharist, engage me all the day, so when rest comes, I may find my sleep in your sweet heart. Amen.

Prayers after Holy Communion

What has passed our lips as food, O Lord, may we possess in purity of heart, that what is given to us in time, be our healing for eternity. May Your Body, O Lord, which I have eaten, and Your Blood which I have drunk, cleave to my very soul, and grant that no trace of sin be found in me, whom these pure and holy mysteries have renewed. Who live and reign, world without end. Amen. We humbly beseech You, almighty god, to grant that those whom You refresh with Your sacraments, may serve you worthily by a life well pleasing to You. Through our

Lord Jesus Christ, Your Son, Who lives and reigns, world without end. Amen.

Dear Lord, help me to remove from my mind every thought or opinion which You would not sanction, every feeling from my heart which You would not approve. Grant that I may spend the hours of the day gladly working with You according to Your will. Help me just for today and be with me in it. In conversations, that they may not be to me occasions of being uncharitable.

In the day's worries and disappointments, that I may be patient with myself and with those around me.

In moments of fatigue and illness, that I may be mindful of others rather than of myself.

In temptations, that I may be generous and loyal, so that when the day is over I may lay it at Your feet, with its successes which are all Yours, and its failures which are all my own, and feel that life is real and peaceful, and blessed when spent with You as the Guest of my soul. Amen.

Before a Crucifix

Look down upon me, good and gentle Jesus, while before Your face I humbly kneel and, with burning soul, pray and beseech You to fix deep in my heart lively sentiments of faith, hope and charity; true contrition for my sins, and a firm purpose of amendment. While I contemplate, with great love and tender pity, your five most precious wounds, pondering over them within me and calling to mind the words which David, Your prophet, said of You, my Jesus: "They have pierced My hands and My feet, they have numbered all My bones. Amen.

After Mass

Lord Jesus Christ, take all my freedom,
my memory, my understanding, and my will.
All that I have and cherish
you have given me. Amen.

Thanksgiving after Mass

Lord, Father all-powerful and ever-living God, I thank You, for even though I am a sinner, your unprofitable servant, not because of my worth but in the kindness of your mercy, You have fed me with the Precious Body & Blood of Your Son, our Lord Jesus Christ. I pray that this Holy Communion may not bring me condemnation and punishment but forgiveness and salvation. May it be a helmet of faith and a shield of good will. May it purify me from evil ways and put an end to my evil passions. May it bring me charity and patience, humility and obedience, and growth in the power to do good. May it be my strong defense against all my enemies, visible and invisible, and the perfect calming of all my evil impulses, bodily and spiritual. May it unite me more closely to you, the One true God, and lead me safely through death to everlasting happiness with You. And I pray that You will lead me, a sinner, to the banquet where you, with Your Son and holy Spirit, are true and perfect light, total fulfillment, everlasting joy, gladness without end, and perfect happiness to your saints. Grant this through Christ our Lord. Amen.

CONFESSION/RECONCILIATION PRAYERS

Prayer before Confession

Receive my confession, O most loving and gracious Lord Jesus Christ, only hope for the salvation of my soul. Grant to me true contrition of soul, so that day and night I may by penance make satisfaction for my many sins. Savior of the world, O good Jesus, Who gave Yourself to the death of the Cross to save sinners, look upon me, most wretched of all sinners; have pity on me, and give me the light to know my sins, true sorrow for them, and a firm purpose of never committing them again.

O gracious Virgin Mary, Immaculate Mother of Jesus, I implore you to obtain for me by your powerful intercession these graces from you Divine Son. Saint Joseph, pray for me. Amen.

Act of Contrition

O my God, I am heartily sorry for having offended you, and I detest all my sins because of your just punishments, but most of all because they offend you, my God, Who are all-good and deserving of all my love. I firmly resolve, with the help of your grace, to sin no more and to avoid the near occasions of sin. Amen.

My God, I am sorry for my sins with all my heart. In choosing to do wrong and failing to do good, I have sinned against you whom I should love above all things. I firmly intend, with your help, to do penance, to sin no more, and to avoid whatever leads me to sin. Our Savior Jesus Christ suffered and died for us. In his name, my God, have mercy. Amen.

O my God, I am sorry for my sins because I have offended you. I know I should love you above all things. Help me to do penance, to do better, and to avoid anything that might lead me to sin. Amen.

After Confession

O almighty and most merciful God, I give You thanks with all the powers of my soul for this and all other mercies, graces, and blessings bestowed on me, and prostrating myself at Your sacred feet, I offer myself to be henceforth forever Yours. Let nothing in life or death ever separate me from You! I renounce with my whole soul all my treasons against You, and all the abominations and sins of my past life. I renew my promises made in Baptism, and from this moment I dedicate myself eternally to Your love and service. Grant that for the time to come, I may detest sin more than death itself, and avoid all such occasions and companies as have unhappily brought me to it. This I resolve to do by the aid of Your divine grace, without which I can do nothing. Amen.

My dearest Jesus, I have told all my sins to the best of my ability. I have sincerely tried to make a good confession and I know that You have forgiven me. Thank You, dear Jesus! Your Divine Heart is full of love and mercy for poor sinners. I love You, dear Jesus; You are so good to me. My loving Savior, I shall try to keep from sin and to love more each day. Dearest Mother Mary, pray for me and help me to keep all my promises. Protect me and do not let me fall back into sin. Dear God, help me to lead a good life. Without Your grace, I can do nothing. Amen.

Reconciliation

Dear Lord Jesus, for the sake of your sorrowful passion, I ask you to forgive all my sins, especially those that have allowed any form of sickness or disease to enter my body and harm my health. I humbly ask you to send forth the Holy Spirit's gift of conviction and shine the light of truth into the deepest recesses of my soul, so that I may make a complete act of contrition before you now.

Lord Jesus, please forgive me for all my sins, especially for any unknown and hidden sins. I am heartily sorry for having offended you. I ask forgiveness for all the times I have failed to make you Lord over my life. Forgive me for placing false gods before you; bowing down and serving idols; for taking your most holy name in vain and for failing to observe the Sabbath day of rest. Please forgive me for not honoring my father and mother, committing the sin of adultery or abortion, stealing, bearing false witness and coveting my neighbor's spouse, property and possessions.

Please forgive me for not loving you with my whole heart, mind, body, soul and spirit, for not loving my neighbor as myself and for disrespecting the temple of your Holy

Spirit. Please forgive me for not taking better care of my health, for eating unhealthy foods and poisoning my body with chemicals, drugs, alcohol, nicotine, caffeine and any other harmful substance or medication.

Please forgive me for committing the sins of hypocrisy, intolerance, unforgiveness, ungratefulness, disbelief, deception, disobedience, envy, pride, fantasy, fornication, idolatry, impatience, division, dissension, offending others, hard-heartedness, hate, haughtiness, anger, rebellion, gambling, greed, intimidation, jealousy, perfectionism, being judgmental, lust, legalism, manipulation, resentment, rudeness, sexual idolatry, sexual immorality, sexual impurity, sexual perversion, selfishness, self-centeredness, self-righteousness, self-pity, slander, worry, vanity, worldliness, witchcraft, addictions, dependencies, complaining, gossiping and all other forms of unrighteousness.

Lord Jesus, I ask you to forgive me for all my sins, trespasses and transgressions and to cover all my offenses with your most precious blood. Surround me with your light and penetrate the very depths of my being with your love. Let no area of darkness remain in me, but transform my whole being

with the healing light of your infinite love.
Amen.

MORNING PRAYERS

Arising from Sleep

O Master and holy God, who are beyond
our understanding: at your word, light came
forth out of darkness. In your mercy, you
gave us rest through night-long sleep, and
raised us up to glorify your goodness and to
offer our supplication to You. Now, in your
own tender love, accept us who adore You
and give thanks to You with all our heart.
Grant us all our requests, if they lead to salvation; give us the grace of manifesting that
we are children of light and day, and heirs
to your eternal reward. In the abundance of
your mercies, O Lord, remember all your
people; all those present who pray with us;
all our brethren on land, at sea, or in the air,
in every place of Your domain, who call upon
your love for mankind. Upon all, pour down
your great mercy, that we, saved in body and
in soul, may persevere unfailingly; and that,
in our confidence, we may extol your exalt-

ed and blessed Name, Father, Son, and Holy Spirit, always, now and forever. Amen.

Fatima Morning Offering

O Jesus, through the Immaculate Heart of Mary, I offer You my prayers, works, joys and sufferings, all that this day may bring, be they good or bad: for the love of God, for the conversion of sinners, and in reparation for all the sins committed against the Sacred Heart of Jesus and the Immaculate Heart of Mary. Amen.

Morning Offering

Most Holy and Adorable Trinity, one God in three Persons, I firmly believe that You are here present; I adore You with the most profound humility; I praise You and give You thanks with all my heart for the favors You have bestowed on me. Your Goodness has brought me safely to the beginning of this day. Behold, O Lord, I offer You my whole being and in particular all my thoughts, words and actions, together with such crosses and contradictions as I may meet with in the course of this day. Give them, O Lord, Your blessing; may Your divine Love animate them and may they tend to the greater honor and glory of Your Sovereign Majesty. Amen.

Morning Offering to the Sacred Heart
O Jesus, through the Immaculate Heart of Mary, I offer You my prayers, works, joys and sufferings of this day for all the intentions of Your Sacred Heart, in union with the Holy Sacrifice of the Mass throughout the world, in reparation for my sins, for the intentions of all our associates, and in particular for the intentions of our Holy Father for this month. Amen.

ADVENT PRAYERS

Come, long-expected Jesus. Excite in me a wonder at the wisdom and power of Your Father and ours. Receive my prayer as part of my service of the Lord who enlists me in God's own work for justice.

Come, long-expected Jesus. Excite in me a hunger for peace: peace in the world, peace in my home, peace in myself.

Come, long-expected Jesus. Excite in me a joy responsive to the Father's joy. I seek His will so I can serve with gladness, singing and love.

Come, long-expected Jesus. Excite in me the joy and love and peace it is right to bring to the manger of my Lord. Raise in me, too, sober reverence for the God who acted there, hearty gratitude for the life begun there, and spirited resolution to serve the Father and Son.

I pray in the name of Jesus Christ, whose advent I hail. Amen.

Father, in the wilderness of the Jordan you sent a messenger to prepare people's hearts for the coming of your Son. Help me to hear his words and repent of my sins, so that I may clearly see the way to walk, the truth to speak, and the life to live for Him, our Lord Jesus Christ. Amen.

All-powerful God, increase our strength of will for doing good that Christ may find an eager welcome at his coming and call us to his side in the kingdom of heaven, where he lives and reigns with you and the Holy Spirit, one God, for ever and ever. Amen.

Father in heaven, our hearts desire the warmth of your love and our minds are searching for the light of your Word. Increase our longing for Christ our Savior and give us the strength to grow in love, that the dawn of his coming may find us rejoicing in his presence and welcoming the light of his truth. We ask this in the name of Jesus the Lord. Amen.

God of power and mercy, open our hearts in welcome. Remove the things that hinder us from receiving Christ with joy, so that we may share his wisdom and become one with him when he comes in glory, for he lives and reigns with you and the Holy Spirit, one God, for ever and ever. Amen.

Father in heaven, the day draws near when the glory of your Son will make radiant the night of the waiting world. May the lure of greed not impede us from the joy which moves the hearts of those who seek him. May the darkness not blind us to the vision of wisdom which fills the minds of those who find him. We ask this in the name of Jesus the Lord. Amen.

Lord God, may we, your people, who look forward to the birthday of Christ experience the joy of salvation and celebrate that feast with love and thanksgiving. We ask this through our Lord Jesus Christ, your Son, who lives and reigns with you and the Holy Spirit, one God, for ever and ever. Amen.

Father of our Lord Jesus Christ, ever faithful to your promises and ever close to your Church: the earth rejoices in hope of the Savior's coming and looks forward with longing to his return at the end of time. Prepare our hearts and remove the sadness that hinders us from feeling the joy and hope which his presence will bestow, for he is Lord for ever and ever. Amen.

Lord, fill our hearts with your love, and as you revealed to us by an angel the coming of your Son as man, so lead us through his suffering and death to the glory of his resurrection, for he lives and reigns with you and the Holy Spirit, one God, for ever and ever. Amen.

Father, all-powerful God, your eternal Word took flesh on our earth when the Virgin

Mary placed her life at the service of your plan. Lift our minds in watchful hope to heart the voice which announces his glory and open our minds to receive the Spirit who prepares us for his coming. We ask this through Christ our Lord. Amen.

CHRISTMAS PRAYERS

Prayer for Christmas Dawn

Father, we are filled with the new light by the coming of your Word among us. May the light of faith shine in our words and actions. Grant this through our Lord Jesus Christ, your Son, who lives and reigns with you and the Holy Spirit, one God, for ever and ever. Amen.

Prayer for Christmas Dawn

Almighty God and Father of light, a child is born for us and a son is given to us. Your eternal Word leaped down from heaven in the silent watches of the night, and now your Church is filled with wonder at the nearness of her God. Open our hearts to receive his life and increase our vision with the rising of dawn, that our lives may be filled with his glory and his peace, who lives and reigns for ever and ever. Amen.

Before Breakfast Prayer for Christmas Season

The Word was made flesh, alleluia, alleluia! And dwelt among us, alleluia, alleluia! Let the heavens rejoice and the earth be glad, before the face of the Lord, for He comes. Bless us, O Lord, and these Thy gifts, which we are about to receive from Thy bounty. Through Christ our Lord. Amen.

Prayer After Breakfast During Christmas Season

Glory to God in the highest, and on earth peace to men of good will, alleluia! The Lord has reigned, and He is clothed with beauty. Almighty God, the Savior of the world, who hast nourished us with heavenly food, we give Thee thanks for the gift of this bodily refreshment which we have received from Thy bountiful mercy. Through Christ our Lord. Amen.

Christmas Prayer

Lord, in this holy season of prayer and song and laughter, we praise you for the great wonders you have sent us: for shining star and angel's song, for infant's cry in lowly manger. We praise you for the Word made flesh in a little Child. We behold his glory, and are bathed in its radiance.

Be with us as we sing the ironies of Christmas, the incomprehensible comprehended, the poetry made hard fact, the helpless Babe who cracks the world asunder. We kneel before you shepherds, innkeepers, wise men. Help us to rise bigger than we are. Amen.

Lord God, we praise you for creating man, and still more for restoring him in Christ. Your Son shared our weakness; may we share his glory, for he lives and reigns with you and the Holy Spirit, one God, for ever and ever. Amen.

God of love, Father of all, the darkness that covered the earth has given way to the bright dawn of your Word made flesh. Make us a people of this light. Make us faithful to your Word, that we may bring your life to the waiting world. Grant this through Christ our Lord. Amen.

Novena

Hail, and blessed be the hour and moment At which the Son of God was born Of a most pure Virgin At a stable at midnight in Bethlehem In the piercing cold At that hour vouchsafe, I beseech Thee, To hear my prayers and grant my desires (mention requests here).

Through Jesus Christ and His most Blessed Mother. Amen.

Vigil Prayer

God our Father, every year we rejoice as we look forward to this feast of our salvation. May we welcome Christ as our Redeemer, and meet him with confidence when he comes to be our judge, who lives and reigns with you and the Holy Spirit, one God, for ever and ever. Amen.

Vigil Prayer

God of endless ages, Father of all goodness, we keep vigil for the dawn of salvation and the birth of your Son. With gratitude we recall his humanity, the life he shared with the sons of men. May the power of his divinity help us answer his call to forgiveness and life. We ask this through Christ our Lord. Amen.

Midnight Mass

Father, you make this holy night radiant with the splendor of Jesus Christ our light. We welcome him as Lord, the true light of the world. Bring us to eternal joy in the kingdom of heaven, where he lives and reigns with you and the Holy Spirit, one God, for ever and ever. Amen.

Midnight Mass

Lord our God, with the birth of your Son, your glory breaks on the world. Through the night hours of the darkened earth, we your people watch for the coming of your promised Son. As we wait, give us a foretaste of the joy that you will grant us when the fullness of his glory has filled the earth, who lives and reigns with you for ever and ever. Amen.

PRAYERS FOR EASTER

Easter Morning

As the world sings triumphant cries to heaven over death that You conquered, help us, Lord, tomorrow as well, when the dresses are put away and the candy is all eaten and on with life we go let us not forget.

The celebration of Your Resurrection over death is a celebration of life that should continue well beyond the sunrise service and the music, rehearsed for days prior; it is beyond the sign of spring beyond the lily beyond new lambs grazing in open fields.

Resurrection is a daily celebration over fear; man's greatest and most powerful enemy. Fear of tomorrow, fear of our yesterdays, fear of what shall become of our young our old our unborn. Resurrection is replacing fear with physical action.

This alone, the most touching and profound of Your signs that fear is dead and belief in You brings, not just hope but life.

What better living parable could You have brought? All fear death. All. Even in the garden, You took on our fear if for only moments, it was as real as our fears can be real and You knew then that this single enemy must be destroyed.

And, You sacrificed Your life, leaving those who had been comfort, and follower; You left them behind, to conquer fear.

I shall cling to this now, and the tomorrows given me.

Peace and Thanksgiving lifted unto You. Amen.

Renewal of Baptismal Promises

Jesus Christ, I acknowledge you as King of the universe. All creation was made for you. Exercise all your sovereign rights over me. I renew my baptismal promises, renouncing Satan and all his works and empty promises, and I promise to lead a good Christian life. I will try to bring about the recognition of the truth of God and your Church. Divine Heart of Jesus, I offer all my actions that every human heart may accept your kingship. May the kingdom of your peace be established across the world. Amen.

"ACTS OF" PRAYERS

Act of Adoration

Jesus, my God, I adore You, here present in the Blessed Sacrament of the altar, where You wait day and night to be our comfort while we await Your unveiled presence in heaven. Jesus, my God, I adore You in all places where the Blessed Sacrament is reserved and where sins are committed against this Sacrament of Love. Jesus, my God, I adore You for all time, past, present and future, for every soul that ever was, is or shall be created. Jesus, my God, who for us has endured hunger and cold, labor and fatigue, I adore You. Jesus, my God, who for my sake has deigned to subject Yourself to the humiliation of temptation, to the perfidy and defection of friends, to the scorn of Your enemies, I adore You. Jesus, my God, who for us has endured the buffeting of Your passion, the scourging, the crowning with thorns, the heavy weight of the cross, I adore You. Jesus, my God, who, for my salvation and that of all mankind, was cruelly nailed to the cross and hung there for three long hours in bitter agony, I adore You. Jesus, My God, who for love of us did institute this Blessed Sacrament and offer Yourself daily for the sins of men, I adore You. Jesus, my God, who in Holy Communion became the food of my soul, I adore You. Jesus, for You I live. Jesus, for You I die. Jesus, I am Yours in life and death. Amen.

Act of Charity

O my God, I love you above all things with my whole heart and soul because you are all good and worthy of all my love.

I love my neighbor as myself for the love of you.

I forgive all who have injured me and ask pardon of all whom I have injured. Amen.

Act of Consecration to Jesus

Lord Jesus Christ, I consecrate myself today anew and without reserve to your divine Heart. I consecrate to you my body with all its senses, my soul with all its faculties, my entire being. I consecrate to you all my thoughts, words and deeds, all my sufferings and labors, all my hopes, consolations and joys. In particular, I consecrate to you this poor heart of mine so that it may love only you and may be consumed as a victim in the fire of your love. Amen.

I place my trust in you without reserve and I hope for the remission of my sins through your infinite mercy. I place within your hands all my cares and anxieties. I promise to love you and to honor you till the last moment of my life, and to spread, as much as I can, devotion to your most Sacred Heart.

Do with me what you will, my Jesus. I deserve no other reward except your greater glory and your holy love. Take this offering of myself and give me a place within your divine Heart forever. Amen.

Act of Consecration to Saint Joseph

O dearest Saint Joseph, I consecrate myself to your honor and give myself to you, that you may always be my father, my protector and my guide in the way of salvation. Obtain for me a greater purity of heart and fervent love of the interior life. After your example may I do all my actions for the greater glory of God, in union with the Divine Heart of Jesus and the Immaculate Heart of Mary. O Blessed Saint Joseph, pray for me, that I may share in the peace and joy of your holy death. Amen.

Act of Consecration to the Holy Ghost

On my knees before the great multitude of heavenly witnesses, I offer myself soul and body to Thee, Eternal Spirit of God. I adore the brightness of Thy purity, the unerring keenness of Thy justice, and the might of Thy love. Thou art the Strength and Light of my soul. In Thee I live and move and am. I desire never to grieve Thee by unfaithfulness to grace, and I pray with all my heart to be kept from the smallest sin against Thee. Mercifully guard my every thought and grant that I may always watch for Thy light and listen to Thy voice and follow Thy gracious inspirations. I cling to Thee and give myself to Thee and ask Thee by Thy compassion to watch over me in my weakness. Holding the pierced Feet of Jesus and looking at His Five Wounds and trusting in His Precious Blood and adoring His opened Side and stricken Heart, I implore Thee Adorable Spirit, helper of my infirmity, so to keep me in Thy grace that I may never sin against Thee. Give me grace O Holy Ghost, Spirit of the

Father and the Son, to say to Thee always and everywhere, Speak Lord, for Thy servant heareth. Amen.

Act of Consecration to the Immaculate Heart of Mary

I, a faithless sinner, renew and ratify today in thy hands, O Immaculate Mother, the vows of my Baptism. I renounce forever Satan, his pomp's and works, and I give myself entirely to Jesus Christ, the Incarnate Wisdom, to carry my cross after Him all the days of my life, and to be more faithful to Him than I have ever been before.

In the presence of all the heavenly court, I choose thee this day for my Mother and Mistress. I deliver and consecrate to thee, as they slave, my body and soul, my goods, both interior and exterior, and even the value of all my good actions, past, present and future, leaving to thee the entire and full right of disposing of me, and all that belongs to me, without exception, according to thy good pleasure, for the greater glory of God, in time and in eternity. Amen.

Saint Louis de Montfort

Act of Consecration to the Immaculate Heart of Mary

O Mary, Virgin most powerful and Mother of Mercy, Queen of Heaven and Refuge of Sinners, we consecrate ourselves to thy Immaculate Heart. We consecrate to thee our very being and our whole life: all that we have, all that we love, all that we are. To thee we give our bodies, our hearts, and our souls; to thee we give our homes, our families and our country. We desire that all that is in us and around us may belong to thee and may share in the benefits of thy motherly blessing. And, that this act of consecration may be truly fruitful and lasting, we renew this day at thy feet the promises of our Baptism and our First Holy Communion. We pledge ourselves to profess courageously and at all times the truths of our holy Faith, and to live as befits Catholics, who are submissive to all directions of the Pope and the bishops in communion with him. We pledge ourselves to keep the Commandments of God and His Church, in particular to keep holy the Lord's Day. We pledge ourselves to make the consoling practices of the Christian religion, and above all, Holy Communion, an important part of our lives, in so far as we shall be able to do. Finally, we promise thee, O glorious Mother of God and loving Mother of men, to devote ourselves whole-heartedly to the spreading of devotion to thy Immaculate Heart, in order to hasten and assure, through the queenly rule of thy Immaculate Heart, the coming of the kingdom of the Sacred Heart of thy adorable Son, in our own hearts and in those of all men, in our country, and in all the world, as in Heaven, so on earth. Amen.

Act of Contrition

O, my God, I am heartily sorry for having offended you. I detest all my sins because of your just punishment, but most of all because they offend you, my God, who are all-good and deserving of all my love. I firmly resolve, with the help of Your grace, to sin no more and to avoid the near occasion of sin. Amen.

Act of Contrition

My God, I am sorry for my sins with all my heart. In choosing to do wrong and failing to do good, I have sinned against you whom I should love above all things. I firmly intend, with your help, to do penance, to sin no more, and to avoid whatever leads me to sin. Our Savior Jesus Christ suffered and died for us. In his name, my God, have mercy. Amen.

Act of Contrition

O my God, I am sorry for my sins because I have offended you. I know I should love you above all things. Help me to do penance, to do better, and to avoid anything that might lead me to sin. Amen.

Act of Contrition

O Lord Jesus, lover of our souls, who, for the great love with which You loved us, willed not the death of a sinner, but rather that he should be converted and live, I grieve from the bottom of my heart that I offended You, my most loving Father and Redeemer, to whom all sin is infinitely displeasing, who so loved that You shed Your blood for me, and endured the bitter torments of a most cruel death. O my God, my infinite Goodness, would that I never offended You. Pardon me, O Lord Jesus, as I most humbly implore Your mercy. Have pity on a sinner for whom Your blood pleads before the face of the Father.

O merciful and forgiving Lord, for the love of Your, I forgive all who have ever offended me. I firmly resolve to forsake and flee from all sins, and to avoid the occasions of them, to confess, in bitterness of spirit, all those sins which I committed against Your divine goodness, and to Love You, O my God, for Your own sake, above all things and forever. Grant me grace so to do, most gracious Lord Jesus. Amen.

Act of Contrition

Merciful Father, I am guilty of sin. I confess my sins before you and I am sorry for them. Your promises are just; therefore, I trust that you will forgive me my sins and cleanse me from every stain of sin. Jesus himself is the proposition for my sins and those of the whole world. I put my hope in his atonement. May my sins be forgiven through his name, and in his blood may my soul be made clean. Amen.

Act of Faith

Lord, I am not worthy that you should enter under my roof, but only say the word and my soul shall be healed.

O my God, I firmly believe that you are one God in three divine persons, Father, Son and Holy Spirit. I believe that your divine Son became man and died for our sins, and that he will come to judge the living and the dead. I believe these and all the truths which the holy catholic Church teaches, because in revealing them you can neither deceive nor be deceived. Amen.

Act of Faith

I believe in one God. I believe that God rewards the good and punishes the wicked. I believe that in God there are three Divine Persons - God the Father, God the Son, and God the Holy Spirit. I believe that God the Son became Man, without ceasing to be God. I believe that he is my Lord and Savior, the Redeemer of the human race, that he died on the Cross for the salvation of all men, that he died also for me.

I believe, on God's authority, everything that he has taught and revealed.

O my God, give me strong faith. O my God, help me to believe with lively faith.

O my God, who are all-good and all-merciful, I sincerely hope to be saved. Help me to do all that necessary for my salvation.

I have committed many sins in my life, but now I turn away from them, and hate them. I am sorry, truly sorry for all of them, because I have offended you, my God, who are all-good, all-perfect, all-holy, all-merciful and kind, and who died on the Cross for me.

I love you, O my God, with all my heart. Please forgive me for having offended you.

I promise, O God, that with your help I will never offend you again.

My God, have mercy on me. Amen.

Act of Faith ...in the Real Presence

My divine Lord, I firmly believe that I am going to receive in Holy Communion your Body, Blood, Soul, and Divinity. I believe this because you have said it, and I am ready to maintain this truth at the peril of my life. Amen.

An Act of Faith, Hope, and Love

Jesus, I believe in you.

Jesus, I hope in you.

Jesus, I love you. Amen.

Act of Hope

O my God, relying on Your almighty power and infinite mercy and promises, I hope to obtain pardon of my sins, the help of Your grace and life everlasting, through the merits of Jesus Christ, my Lord and Redeemer. Amen.

Act of Hope

For your mercies' sake, O Lord my God, tell me what you are to me. Say to my soul: "I am your salvation." So speak that I may hear, O Lord; my heart is listening; open it that it may hear you, and say to my soul: "I am your salvation." After hearing this word, may I come in haste to take hold of you. Hide not your face from me. Let me see your face even if I die, lest I die with longing to see it. The house of my soul is too small to receive you; let it be enlarged by you. It is all in ruins; do you repair it. There are things in it - I confess and I know - that must offend your sight.

But who shall cleanse it? Or to what others besides you shall I cry out? From my secret sins cleanse me, O Lord, and from those of others spare your servant. Amen.

Saint Augustine of Hippo

Act of Humility

O divine Lord, how shall I dare to approach you, I who have so often offended you? No, Lord, I am not worthy that you should enter under my roof; but speak only the word and my soul shall be healed. Amen.

Act of Love

O my God, I love You above all things with my whole heart and soul, because you are all-good and worthy of all love. I love my neighbor as myself for the love of You. I forgive all who have injured me and ask pardon of all whom I have injured. Amen.

Act of Love

O God, all that I am and all that I have is from you. You have given me my gifts of body and soul. You have numbered me among your favored children. You have showered me with countless graces and blessings. From all eternity you have thought of me and loved me. How shall I ever love you in return?

And now in your merciful goodness you are coming into my soul to unit yourself most intimately with me. You came into the world for love of man, but now you are coming from the altar for love of me. You are coming to fill me heart with your holy love, my Creator, my Redeemer, my Sanctifier, my God.

O Jesus, I want to return this love. I want to love you with all the powers of my soul. I want to belong only to you, to consecrate myself to you alone. Jesus, let me live for you; let me die for you. Living and dying may I be yours. Amen.

Act of Love

O my divine Jesus, how shall I return you thanks for the goodness in giving yourself to me? The only way I can repay your love is by loving you in return. Yes, my Lord, I love you, and I desire to love you all my life.

My Jesus, you alone are sufficient for me. Whom shall I love, if I love not you, my Jesus? You love those who love you. I love you. Oh, do you also love me. If I love you but little, give me the love which you require of me.

O Mary, my good Mother, and you glorious Saint Joseph, lend me your love wherewith to love my Jesus. Amen.

Act of Oblation to the Sacred Heart

My loving Jesus, out of the grateful love I bear you, and to make reparation for my unfaithfulness to grace, I give you my heart, and I consecrate myself wholly to you; and with your help I purpose never to sin again. Amen.

Act of Offering

O my divine Lord, I offer you my body and its senses, my soul and its faculties, my heart and its sentiments. My thoughts, me desires, my words, my actions, my whole being are yours. Since you have given yourself wholly to me, can I do less than give myself wholly to you? Grant me, O divine Jesus, to persevere in your holy love. Give me a still greater sorrow for my past sins, and strengthen the sincere resolution I have formed never again to offend you. Amen.

Act of Petition

Give me yourself, O my God, give yourself to me. Behold I love you, and if my love is too weak a thing, grant me to love you more strongly. I cannot measure my love to know how much it falls short of being sufficient, but let my soul hasten to your embrace and never be turned away until it is hidden in the secret shelter of your presence. This only do I know, that it is not good for me when you are not with me, when you are only outside me. I want you in my very self. All the plenty in the world which is not my God is utter want. Amen.

Saint Augustine of Hippo

Act of Resignation

O Lord, my God, from this day I accept from your hand willingly and with submission, the kind of death that it may please you to send me, with all its sorrows, pains, and anguish. Into your hands, O Lord, I commend my spirit. Amen.

Act of Spiritual Communion

My Jesus, I believe that Thou art present in the Blessed Sacrament. I love Thee above all things and I desire Thee in my soul. Since I cannot now receive Thee sacramentally, come at least spiritually into my heart. As though thou wert already there, I embrace Thee and unite myself wholly to Thee; permit not that I should ever be separated from Thee. Amen.

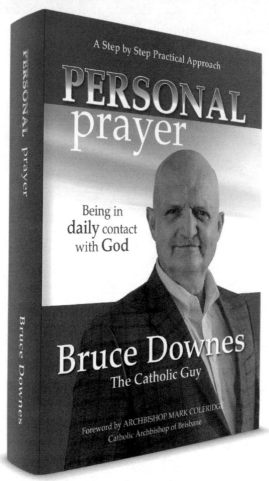